CENTER FOR ORIGINS RESEARCH

IN CREATION

Johannes Buteo's The Shape and Capacity of Noah's Ark

Translated by

Timothy Griffith and Natali H. Monnette

with an introduction by

Todd Charles Wood

Center for Origins Research Issues in Creation
Number 2
February 29, 2008

WIPF & STOCK · Eugene, Oregon

JOHANNES BUTEO'S THE SHAPE AND CAPACITY OF NOAH'S ARK

ISBN 13: 978-1-55635-871-5

www.wipfandstock.com

Abstract

Sixteenth century French mathematician Johannes Buteo published an influential logistical study of Noah's Ark in 1554. The treatise *Arca Noë, Cuius Formae, Capacitatisque Fuerit, Libellus* originally appeared as part of his *Opera Geometrica*. This was the first work to seriously consider the logistical details of the Ark, including its construction, capacity, and an estimation of the number of inhabitants and food and provisions required. Other logistical studies of Noah's Ark appeared in the 150 years following Buteo's work, and all based their innovations on Buteo's pioneering study. Presented here for the first time is Buteo's entire work in English.

Contents

Johannes Buteo, Accommodation, and the Integration of Faith and Learning

Todd Charles Wood

The sixteenth century is notable in Europe for the rejection of traditional knowledge in favor of empirical observation. After studying the Bible, Martin Luther clashed with Catholic authority over its meaning and application. In the area of natural philosophy, 1543 was a particularly important year, with the publication of Copernicus' correction of Aristotle's cosmology and of Vesalius' correction of Galen's anatomy.[1]

For most scientists today, the struggle between authority and free inquiry is personified in Galileo's struggle with the Catholic church over the Copernican cosmology at the beginning of the seventeenth century. In his *Letter to the Grand Duchess Christina*, Galileo outlined a hermeneutical tactic that he believed answered the biblical objections to Copernicanism. According to Galileo,

> I think that in discussions of physical problems we ought to begin not from the authority of scriptural passages but from sense-experiences and necessary demonstrations.... It is necessary for the Bible, in order to be accommodated to the understanding of every man, to speak many things which appear to differ from the absolute truth so far as the bare meaning of the words is concerned. But Nature, on the other hand, is inexorable and immutable; she never transgresses the laws imposed upon her.... For that reason it appears that nothing physical which sense-experience sets before our eyes, or which necessary demonstrations prove to us, ought to be called in question (much less condemned) upon the testimony of biblical passages which may have some different meaning beneath their words.[2]

This principle of accommodation afforded Galileo a means of explaining biblical passages such as Ps. 104:5, "the foundations of the earth ... should not be removed for ever." According to Galileo, this verse and others like it were not meant to communicate literal truth but rather to

1 Copernicus (1543) and Vesalius (1543).

2 Drake (1957, pp. 182-183).

frame religious revelation in terms that the even the simplest child could understand. The *Letter* failed to convince church authorities and instead provoked the official condemnation of Copernicus by the Inquisition. In Protestant countries, however, Galileo became a popular symbol of authoritarianism run amok, and his principle of accommodation became increasingly popular.

Once the scholarly world adopted accommodation as a justification for doing science without regard to scriptural teaching, the erosion of biblical and religious authority was inevitable. Accommodation produced an imbalanced relationship between religion and natural philosophy. Though the findings of natural philosophy could be used to reinterpret revelation, revelation could not be used to reinterpret natural philosophy. In the words of Royal Society founder John Wilkins, "the demonstrations of astronomy, they are as infallible as truth itself."[3] Gone was the authority of the church, and empiricism took its place. To be sure, there were many attempts to reassert scriptural authority over the centuries that followed, most notably by the scriptural geologists and the antievolutionists, but their protests won no wide appeal.[4] For good or ill, the Galileo affair ensured that accommodation was here to stay.

Amidst the intellectual upheaval of the Renaissance and Enlightment, the work of Johannes Buteo, particularly the work presented here, *De Arca Noë, Cuius Formae, Capacitatisque Fuerit, Libellus*, occupies a forgotten middle ground. He practiced the new rationality based on empiricism, but he employed it to defend the traditional authority of the Bible. He disagreed with some traditional authorities (particularly Origen) but accepted others (Pliny) uncritically. Even in his disagreements, he accepted the broader authority of the literal reading of the Flood story as true history. His treatment of Noah's Ark is not notable for any dramatic scholarly advances, but it exemplifies the gradual development from traditional to empirical knowledge. He also typifies a way of thinking about the Bible and natural philosophy that had not yet yielded to accommodation. Buteo practiced Augustine's admonition,

> I have learned that we should not hesitate to give the answers that have to be given, in line with the faith, to people who make every effort to discredit the books our salvation depends on. So we should show that whatever they have been able to demonstrate from reliable sources about the world of nature is not contrary to our literature, while whatever they may have produced from any of their volumes that is contrary to this literature of ours, that is, to the Catholic faith, we must

3 Wilkins (1802, p. 255).

4 *E.g.*, see Lynch (2002) and Roberts (1988).

either show with some ease, or else believe without any hesitation, to be entirely false.[5]

Originally published in 1554, *Arca Noë* was the first pamphlet in Buteo's *Opera Geometrica*, covering a brief 24 printed pages. Buteo touched on the shape, construction, and capacity of the Ark, numbered the inhabitants, and estimated the amount of provisions required. His work inspired later writers on the same subject, including John Wilkins,[6] Athanasius Kircher,[7] Jeremiah Drexel,[8] and Gaspar Schott.[9] Printed discussions of Noah's Ark continued to use Buteo's calculations and conventions through the eighteenth and early nineteenth centuries. Only with the growing popularity of John Pye Smith's local flood interpretation[10] is Buteo's version of the Ark forgotten.

Buteo's Life and Works

Little is known about Buteo himself, and the surviving biographical accounts differ in significant details.[11] Buteo was born Jean Bourrel (or Borrel) around 1490 in the village of Charpey in the southeastern French region of Dauphiné (Figure 1). One of twenty siblings, Bourrel entered the order of St. Anthony of Vienne to relieve his family of the financial burden of caring for him. At the age of sixteen or seventeen, he moved to St. Antoine l'Abbaye, just seventeen miles from his birthplace, where he became known for his skill in invention and construction of musical instruments. He excelled at learning, especially at mathematics, and spent time in Paris after his thirtieth birthday, where he attended lectures of the French mathematician Oronce Finé. Homesick for the foothills of the Alps, he returned to St. Antoine l'Abbaye. His Latin name Buteo came from a hawk called *bourrel* by the residents of Dauphiné. Prior to the outbreak of the French Wars of Religion, he jointly administered the abbey with Aimar Falco for two years.

Biographical accounts disagree on the time and manner of his death. According to Jacques Auguste de Thou's 1696 account, Buteo died in 1564, soon after the outbreak of the French Wars of Religion. Huguenot fighting in Dauphiné forced him to leave his work and books at the abbey and evacuate ten miles away to Catholic-held Romans-sur-

5 Augustine, *Literal Meaning of Genesis*, I, 41.
6 Wilkins (1668, pp. 162-168).
7 Kircher (1675).
8 Drexel (1640).
9 Schott (1677), cited by Allen (1963, p. 80).
10 Smith (1840).
11 In chronological order of publication, I have consulted biographies by Chorier (1672, p. 540), de Thou and Teissier (1696, pp. 248-249), Bibliotheque Raisonée (1739, pp. 150-151), Bayle (1740, pp. 280-281), de Thou (1740, p. 493), Allard (1797, p. 86), Moreri (1759, pp. 89-90), Montucla (1799, pp. 574-575), Michaud (1812, p. 589), Hoeffer (1855, p. 898-899), and Verdonk (1981).

Figure 1. Principle locations of Buteo's life.

Isère, where he died of grief and boredom. Louis Moreri claimed that Buteo's death, as recorded in the records of the abbey, occurred in 1572. Moreri agreed with de Thou that Buteo fled to Romans-sur-Isère due to the Huguenots, who ransacked the abbey in 1562 and 1567. Historian Nicholas Chorier gave a very different version of Buteo's death in 1560, which would be prior to the outbreak of war.[12] He claimed that Buteo died at the abbey and no mention of the war was made. Huguenot Pierre Bayle elaborated Chorier's account in the 1739 *Bibliothèque Raisonnée*, where he claimed that a Severin Bourrel from Romans-sur-Isère died of grief during the civil wars. According to Bayle, de Thou and Moreri must have confused Jean Bourrel with Severin Bourrel, and therefore the Huguenots were not guilty of causing his death.

It is unclear which account of Buteo's death is correct, either has some merit. De Thou's reputation as a historian would seem to speak in favor of his account, and Bayle's desire to exonerate the Huguenots is an obvious motive for changing the details of Buteo's death. Nevertheless, Chorier's account of Buteo's life, published prior to any other, records simply, "Il mourut dans Saint Antoine l'an M. DLx. âgé de soixante-quinze ans."[13]

12 Bayle (1740).
13 Chorier (1672, p. 540)

Because Buteo had no students or disciples, his notoriety comes entirely from his publications. He did not begin publishing his works until he was around 60 years old. His works consist of three original books, *Opera Geometrica* (1554), *Logistica* (1559), and *De quadratura circuli* (1559). In addition to these, he translated a Greek liturgical work into Latin as *Orationes Graecorum veteres ad Deum et Sanctos* (1558). Verdonk also listed his 1562 *Apologia adversus epistolam Jacobi Peletarii depravatoris Elementorum Euclidis*, and Moreri claimed that Buteo wrote many unpublished manuscripts.

In addition to *Arca Noë*, *Opera Geometrica* contains fourteen other short works on logistics, mechanics, and other topics. Of particular interest is a section on mathematics for legal issues, such as surveying and inheritance. He also refuted Finé's alleged solution to the classic geometric problem of the quadrature of the circle and Micheal Stifel's proposed solution of the duplication of a cube. Buteo treated the quadrature problem again in his 1559 *De quadratura circuli*. *Logistica* covers problems of mathematics and algebra.

During his lifetime, he was recognized as a capable mathematician by Girolamo Maggi,[14] and in 1660 Gerardus Joannes Vossius cited his work in his *De quatuor artibus popularibus*.[15] Verdonk speculated that his sharp criticism of opponents (in *Arca Noë*, Buteo says they "are from your father Satan") might have been a reason for his isolation.[16] More recently, Buteo has been occasionally cited by historians of mathematics,[17] but his chief claim to fame in the modern world is *Arca Noë*.[18] Norman Cohn and Don Cameron Allen both discuss Buteo in

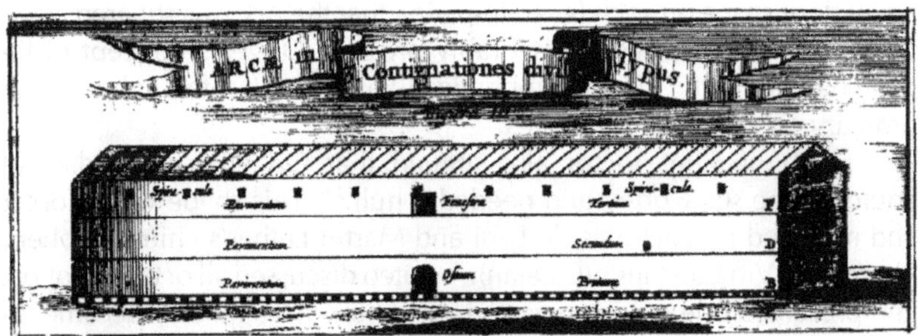

Figure 2. Diagram from Kircher's *Arca Noë* (1675, p. 38), showing that his proposed design of Noah's Ark was adapted from Buteo.

14 Maggi (1564, p. 171).

15 Vossius (1660, p. 300).

16 Verdonk (1981).

17 *E.g.* Cantor (1900, pp. 561-563), Karpinski and Kokomoor (1928), Kokomoor (1928), and Kloyda (1937).

18 *E.g.* Allen (1963, pp. 78-79), Cummings (1972, p. 73), Young (1995, pp. 56-57), Cohn (1996, pp. 40-41), Woodmorappe (1996, p. xiii), and Wood (2007).

their influential works on Noah, from whom others who write on this topic have discovered Buteo's work.

Noah's Ark

Historical interpretations of the account of Noah's Ark illustrate the change in biblical exegesis wrought by accommodation. Prior to Buteo, theologians used a variety of methods to interpret scripture, which can be seen in Hugh of St. Victor's twelfth century *De Arca Noe Morali*. Hugh attends to the shape and size of the Ark, treating it as a real boat and exegeting the account of Noah as literal history. Hugh also extensively discusses the symbolic or typological meaning of the Ark, "... the Church is herself the ark, which her Noah, our Lord Jesus Christ, the Helmsman and the Haven, is guiding through the tempests of this present life, and leading through Himself unto Himself." Typological and literal interpretations were common prior to the Enlightment.

Buteo's work marks a turning point. Absent is the mystical symbolism of Hugh's interpretation. He writes exclusively of what many consider to be the mundane details: how the Ark was built, how many animals it held, how much food it carried. Extensive passages discuss the disagreement between Origen and Augustine on the shape of the Ark and Origen's strange geometrical cubit. Origen believed that the cubit was a geometrical or Egyptian cubit, containing six of the ordinary cubits or nine feet.[19] He also took the Septuagint's translation of Genesis 6:16 to indicate that the peak of the Ark was one square cubit, making the Ark a pyramid.[20] Thus, Origen's version of the Ark would have been a pyramid 270 feet high, 450 feet wide, and 2700 feet (slightly more than half a mile) long. Augustine, in contrast, described an Ark with equal floor space on each level, implying that the Ark was squared rather than pyramidal, though he favorably presents Origen's concept of the geometrical cubit.[21] Buteo emphatically asserted that the cubit was an ordinary cubit of only 18 inches.

Hugh of Saint Victor also argued that Origen's pyramidal Ark could not be sea-worthy and needed a hull.[22] This shape was adopted and modified by Nicholas de Lyra and Martin Luther's chief opponent, Thomas de Vio Caietanus (Cajetan).[23] Buteo discussed all of these options and presented one of his own: a squared box. This quickly became the most popular perception of the Ark's design (Figure 2) and can still be seen in modern works.[24]

19 *Homilies on Genesis*, II.
20 *Homilies on Genesis*, II.
21 *City of God* 15.27.
22 *De Arca Noe Morali* 1.12.
23 *Commentarii: et primum in Genesim*, chapter VI (Caietani 1639, p. 43); see also Allen (1963, pp. 75-76).
24 *E.g.*, Cummings (1972, pp. 75-76) and Navarra (1974, p. 114).

In contrast to his critical appraisal of Origen's Ark, Buteo relied uncritically on Pliny when dealing with the capacity of the Ark. Among the animals aboard, Buteo listed unicorns and pegasus. Buteo also introduced an approximation that became popular. Instead of speaking in terms of precise space and food requirements, Buteo related each animal to its approximate equivalent in sheep, oxen, or wolves. Thus, Buteo assumed "that two elephants would be equivalent to eight cows in terms of space and food required." He concluded that Noah's Ark required space for 120 oxen, 80 sheep, and 80 wolves (with an additional 3650 sheep to feed the carnivores).

Buteo's literal approach to interpretation of Genesis became a model for future interpreters of Noah's Ark.[25] His simplification of the Ark capacity problem endured to the nineteenth century in the 1832 English edition of *Calmet's Dictionary*, in which Buteo's precise numbers are noted (without citation) as the capacity needs of the Ark.[26] While the literalistic interpretation of Noah's Ark endured, other literal interpretations fell by the wayside. The Flood itself was called into question by John Pye Smith, and the emerging science of geology seemed to imply that the earth was much older than the biblical chronology might indicate. More and more frequently, accommodation was invoked to explain why science seemed to contradict the plain meaning of the Bible. Today, only young-age creationists carry on the tradition of literally interpreting Genesis, and they continue to produce logistical studies of Noah's Ark,[27] unwittingly following precedents set by Buteo four hundred years ago.

Beyond the minutiae of ark logistics, what significance does Buteo have for modern creationism? Buteo's approach to scripture would seem to be a productive one for creationists to emulate. He actively integrates his faith with learning, a topic of great interest in the faculty meetings of many Christian colleges. He does not allow science to have the final word, nor does he allow historical interpretations to have unchallenged authority. He carefully sifts interpretations without abandoning his commitment to the authority of scripture. Buteo's strategy for integrating science and faith fosters mutual development of both, rather than the domination of one over the other. Modern creationists who desire to practice critical science within a carefully-exegeted understanding of Genesis would do well to follow Buteo's lead.[28]

---

25 See Rex (1976).
26 Taylor (1832, p. 94).
27 *E.g.*, Woodmorappe (1996).
28 *E.g.*, Brand (2006).

Johannes Buteo's The Shape and Capacity of Noah's Ark

Translation Note

The following translation and transcription of Buteo's *Arca Noë, Cuius Formae, Capacitatisque Fuerit, Libellus* comes from the 1559 printing of *Opera Geometrica* printed by Michaëlem Iovium in Lyons. Clarifying notes and biblical references have been added to the text in square brackets. Figures are traced from the originals and appear in the same orientation and approximately the same location as in the 1559 printing. Figure legends have been added to the translation for clarity and do not appear in the original. All footnotes were compiled and written by Stephanie Mace of the Center for Origins Research at Bryan College. Original page numbers in the transcription appear in slashes (//) at the beginning of the pages in the 1559 printing.

Johannes Buteo

The Shape and Capacity of Noah's Ark

1. Introduction

Scholars have frequently debated the size and nature of the ark that preserved animal kind from the world destroyed in the Flood, was built by the architect Noah as God commanded, and was recorded by the Prophet Moses. They have debated so much so, in fact, that there is no agreement as to its shape or capacity. Each interprets its description differently, even though the words of the Scriptures themselves are quite plain and easy to understand. But there is some difficulty, arising from some confusion about the units of measurement, which poses a problem even to those who go about understanding it correctly. For heretics, however, it puts them in a fog, as it were, so that in undertaking such a difficult problem, they see nothing but opportunity to deride the Scriptures. Many good Catholics have fallen into the opposite error, rejecting such rubbish by believing that the story of the Flood is true (which it is, of course), rather than by actually understanding it. I shall demonstrate how these same Catholics have grossly exaggerated the size of the ark; and I shall do so using the most convincing argument, that is, geometry. Which, as Cicero himself has said, does not persuade so much as prove.[28] In this way, therefore, I shall come to the aid of our own so I may show them how to refute such heretical arguments with science and character rather than with exaggerated numbers. For it will be better to argue more convincingly this way and win.

2. The description of the ark according to translators

Let us then first hear our Lord in heaven give the measurements of the ark to his foreman Noah. "Make for yourself," He said, "an ark out of smoothed beams."

---

28 Buteo may be referring to "It is like geometry, where if you grant the premises then you must grant everything." (*On Moral Ends*, 5.83.)

> In the ark you shall make chambers, and you shall cover it inside and out with pitch. And you shall make it thus: the length of the ark shall be three hundred cubits, its width fifty cubits, and its height thirty cubits. You shall make a window in the ark, and you shall finish its peak in one cubit. You shall put a door, however, in the ark from the side, you shall make in it below a second story and a third floor.

And so on. This is the common translation.[29] The Greek Septuagint however renders it thus:

> Ποίησεις οὖν σεαυτῷ κιβωτὸν ἐκ ξύλων τετραγώνων. νοσσιὰς ποιήσεις κατ᾽ τὴν κιβωτὸν, καὶ ἀσφαλτώσεις αὐτωὴν ἔσωθεν, καὶ ἔξωθεν τῇ ἀσφάλτῳ, καὶ οὕτω ποιήσεις τὴν κιβωτόν. τριακοσίων πήχεων τὸ μῆκος τῆς κιβωτοῦ, καὶ πεντήκοντα πήχεων τὸ πλάτος, καὶ τριάκοντα πήχεων τὸ ὕψος αὐτῆς. θυείδα ποιήσεις κατ᾽ τὴν κιβωτὸν, καὶ είς πῆ χεων συντελέσεις αὐτὴν ἄνωθεν, τὴν δέ θύραν τῆς κιβωτοῦ ποιήσεις ἐκ πλαγίων. κατάγαια διώφορα καὶ τριώφορα ποιήσεις κατ᾽ αὐτήν.

I have translated this into Latin as follows:

> You yourself shall make therefore an ark for yourself out of squared beams. You shall make dwellings in the ark, and you shall make the ark inside and out with pitch. The length of the ark shall be three hundred cubits, and the width fifty cubits, and the height thirty cubits. You shall make a window in the ark, and you shall finish it on top in one cubit. You shall make the door, however, off the slant. You shall make storerooms of two stories and three stories in it.

And such are the instructions for building the ark. Recently, some have compared the sense of this interpretation with the original Hebrew (as they say) and have discovered it to be accurate in so many words. In the following treatise I will make mention of these whenever it seems appropriate.

3. Explanation and application of the instructions for building the ark

In the very beginning of the description of the structure, it is most enlightening that the proper name and basic shape ascribed to it is *arca* (chest). Nothing could have been easier to understand than this. For a

29 *I.e.*, Vulgate

chest is a thing used by men frequently and known to everybody. Things are enclosed in a chest that we wish to be hidden or kept safe. Varro even thought that it was so named because thieves were "kept out" of a closed chest.[30,31] And although chests come in various sizes depending on what they are being used for (some are for storing clothes, some for money, others for foodstuffs), the same basic shape is found in all chests, except that they vary in the kind of lids that cover them. The lids can be plain and flat, or convex (which is properly termed *vaulted*), such as might be seen in larger chests (which Ulpian called "vaulties" because of their lids[32]) and also in smaller chests, such as are frequently used on pack-mules. But others, such as grain boxes, which the poor use to store grain in, are covered in tapered lids. In all other respects the shape of the actual body of the chest is the same in every type: planes joined together at right angles to form length, width, and depth. This shape is called a parallelepiped rectangle by geometricians. I do not think anyone has ever doubted that the Ark of the Covenant was constructed in this same shape, although in its description its shape is not explained other than the use of the word for chest, which in every place in scripture is rendered *Aron* in Hebrew, although this of ours is always *Teva*. Teachers of Hebrew always claim that these two words are synonymous. Furthermore, the translators of the Septuagint indiscriminately put "κιβωτὸν" for *Aron* and *Teva*, and Latin translators render it *arca*. It is however convenient and clearest to designate any shape by comparing it to something that cannot possibly be misunderstood. Vitruvius does this when discussing hydraulic machines as well as in several other places. He says that a chest should be made from bronze; and he, a man extremely familiar with technical vocabulary, does not go on any further to explain an otherwise difficult concept.[33] But in other places, when there is no convenient comparison, he explains a shape using technical terminology. We see another example in Exodus where the altar is described. It was to be five cubits in length and five cubits in width; then it was added that it was to be a *quadrangle*. But the Greek version renders it even clearer: "τετράγωνον ἔσαι τὸ θυσιαστήριον," that is, "the altar shall be a square." For unless he had remembered that it was to be a square, it could have been interpreted to have the shape of a rhombus. A rhombus of course is made of four equal sides but not at right angles, as it is defined by geometricians. From this, therefore, we can plainly see that no shape can be attributed to the ark (given the literal sense of the words and the name given to the ark) other than the rectangular parallelepiped mentioned above. According to the measurements given to us, its length was six times the width and ten times the height. Even some who are in error

30 *arca* is Latin for "chest"; *arcēre* Latin for "keep out"

31 *De Lingua Latina, Book* 5 §128.

32 Unable to locate instance where Ulpian calls chests "vaulties"

33 *The Architecture of Marcus Vitruvius Pollio in Ten Books,* 10.13.

have come to this same conclusion, as I shall demonstrate at the end of this treatise.

4. The material of the ark

After determining the shape of the ark, we should examine its material, which the Hebrew version establishes as "made from gopher wood." But even Jewish translators (whom we call Rabbis using their own word) are at such a loss as to how the word *gopher* should be interpreted that nothing certain can be known of its definition. For some suggest pine; some, fir; others, cypress; and still others, cedar. Scholars of the Talmud say it is four species of cedar. The one thing that they all can agree on is that *gopher* should be understood as some type of tree. I, however, think this unlikely since it is hardly possible that one region could supply enough lumber from one species to suffice for such a large construction. Furthermore, one kind of wood would not have been the most effective to use in every part of the ark, as trees vary considerably in quality. Some are particularly well-suited for long beams due to their solidity. (These would be especially appropriate for the base.) But others acquired for their lighter nature are excellent to use on roofs. Still others are especially good for flooring and floor joists. Some are recommended for finish material and more detailed work since they are so easily handled. The translators of the Septuagint (as I mentioned above) render this passage, "from squared wood"; our version however translates it, "from smoothed wood." These practically mean the same thing. For when timber is hewn into squares, it certainly could be called *smoothed*, but it is not so specific nor as clear as *squared*. Indeed this design corresponds surprisingly well with the construction of the ark. In fact, it is completely necessary. For I cannot see any way that a structure of that size would be seaworthy and capable of carrying anything, unless the entirety (except for the interior parts) was constructed with squared beams and posts positioned as frequently as possible and with braces tightly joined between them. It would also add much to their strength if the timber were treated with bitumen.

5. The nature of bitumen

The nature of bitumen (as Pliny writes) is similar to that of sulfur: in some places semi-solid; in others, solid.[34] A semi-solid form of bitumen comes from a lake in Palestine that is called Asphaltites from *asphalt*, the Greek word for bitumen; the lake produces nothing else useful. The solid form is found in Syria near the sea port Sidon. Both of these types

34 *The Natural History of Pliny*, 6.35.51.

condense and form clods. Likewise, Joppe in Syria (as Vitruvius says) and Arabia of the Numidians are enormous lakes that produce large amounts of bitumen.[35] And there also are several quarries of hardened bitumen. In its natural state it can be viscous, watery, or oily in Sicily (where it poisons the river from the Acragantine spring); and the inhabitants use it to light their lamps instead of oil. Otherwise, it is used on bronze vessels to make them more resistant to fire. It is also applied in blacksmith shops to iron and nail heads. In addition, since bitumen is resistant to water, it prevents wood from absorbing harmful moisture, preventing rot from penetrating the wood, and keeping out moths, worms, and termites. These qualities make it so especially effective in making things durable. But it also has the particular property of gluing things together: not just wood, but even flesh. For it causes the skin to mend in wounds, and it can join muscles. It was also used for mortar by Queen Semiramides when she was building the walls of Babylon out of brick. Therefore, since these qualities are so well-suited to the construction of the ark, I suspect that the whole sides of the joints were smeared with bitumen as they were being put together, as well as the entire inside of the ark, not just the faces of the beams inside and out. This would not only serve to form tight connections, but also to give it durability while it was still in construction before the cataclysm began. According to the historian Josephus, even after the flood some of the [ark's] remnants (on Mount Cordico in Armenia, where the ark settled as the waters were receding) lasted to his own time, and the name *disembarking* (that is from the disembarking of Noah) remains associated with the place.[36] And even by the most conservative calculation you will find that there were more than 3,000 years from the Flood to Josephus.

6. The ark's window

When it is said, "You shall make a window in the ark," it seems that this repetition is not unnecessary here, but merely to provide that no one think that the window should be located on the roof (as some have mistakenly thought that it was like those now so commonly seen in the roof-tiles on houses). For the ark would necessarily have had a roof due to the continual rainy condition of the sky for forty days. This also is perfectly evident from the context when it is said, "Noah opening the ark's roof." Furthermore, there have been a few among the Jewish Rabbis who would like the window here to be nothing other than a lamp made out of one of the larger gemstones, such as lichnite or carbuncle, that would have lit up the entire ark by the brightness of the shining stone. But this shameless lie is clearly exposed by the passage that immediately

35 *Architecture of Vitruvius,* 8.3.

36 *The Antiquities of the Jews,* 1.3.5.

follows: "Noah, opening the window that he had made, sent out a raven." Others, however, seeing that it would be impossible for the light of a single opening to suffice for the entire body of the ark and all its compartments, claim that windows were placed in a number of places in the ark, but that this particular window was the largest and, as such, was the only one included in God's command. Many of our own have fled to this interpretation and with no inquiry have let it be accepted by the public. But I say there is no need for the ark to have been lighted at all, except only the part where people lived, which in the opinion of all scholars was in the very top of the ark. For we see that wild animals and every kind of reptile not only are not averse to darkness, but by some instinct always seek it out and remain there unless hunger drives them out to look for food. Some even dig out holes for themselves in several places, for which nature has given them sharp claws and the know-how to do it. Others seek out caverns and inaccessible caves; and if they cannot find them, they construct shelters for themselves by heaping up bushes and brush, which are impenetrable even to rain (if you believe Pliny).[37] Some crawl into hollowed out trees. In short, all wild things like the darkness of dens and rest there especially, and as if they hated light, they hide there for entire days and come out only at night. Even domesticated livestock (free-range and those kept in the stable) have no preference for light; they graze better in the dark. Moreover, the birds, which Nature has given the sky, prefer to live mostly in the woods, leafy hedges, and shady places of ravines, unless they fly out to find food. Furthermore, every kind of eagle and hawk, which are the very wildest kind of bird, is tamed by nothing more than darkness. Immediately after capture, fowlers sew their eyelids shut for a few days; and after the birds have been tamed in this fashion (especially those which they call "soaring bird"), they cover their heads in leather hoods with nothing but their beaks sticking out so they cannot see. And when their eyes are covered in this way, they hang on the arm, forget their natural wildness, and remain perfectly calm as they are carried about. But it has been established by nature that animals other than man are able to see to a certain degree even at night and in darkness. Hence, those who unnecessarily and contrary to the Lord's instructions propose additional windows in the ark seem to have foolishly fallen into this error due to ignorance of Nature. To say that only one of many windows was included in God's command, since it was to be the largest, would be just as absurd as to say that several Arks were built by God's command, but that there was only mention of one of them since it was the largest. Nothing is written concerning the measurement of the window, unless someone might think (as some in our own time have recently stated in their notes on the Hebrew text) the following: that "and you shall complete its height in a cubit" refers to the

37 *Natural History*, 2.8.54.

size of the actual window, because of the ambiguous reference in the pronoun *its*, either to the ark or to the window, both of which words are placed nearby. Likewise, the Greek version is ambiguous in the pronoun "αὐτὴν" referring to the window. Although in Greek translations the passage is read incorrectly, having the participle "ἐπισυνάγων," where it should be "θυείδα," that is, *window*. For then the literal sense would be "while gathering or joining you shall make in the ark." Who does not see that this is absurd? And thus the window would be removed from the ark entirely. But the Hebrew word *Thecalena* immediately clears up this ambiguity: the last syllable joined to the word *Thecale* (you shall complete) is "na," a feminine pronoun meaning *her*; this of course cannot be referring to *Soer* (window) as *Soer* is always said to be of the masculine gender. And if it were possible for it to refer to *Soer*, it would have had to have been said *Thecalenu*. Furthermore the word for "you shall complete" or "you shall finish" lends itself to something already begun but not yet finished. This of course is the ark, which was incomplete until it had a covering (*i.e.*, a roof). And you will find no instructions concerning the roof other than in these words. I along with everyone else understand the ark being completed in a cubit to mean that that cubit was to be the height of the middle of the roof along the entire length of the three hundred cubits except for the eaves. This height of course was sufficient for water run-off even for a larger area, particularly if the flat parts were planed and covered in asphalt. In fact, Vitruvius himself only recommends a slope one two-hundredth of the total length in the bottom of a stream where water was lead through artificial canals.[38] But in this configuration, the one-cubit gable of the roof exceeds Vitruvius' recommendation by eight times. Besides this, the rain water and spray falling from every which direction would slide off by its own weight much easier than what would travel through a stream or canal. Therefore, the top of the ark was constructed in the method I have just described at the height of one cubit, but with no width left in the peak, though everyone I have read on this subject would have its width be one cubit as well. Therefore the structure of the ark has been imagined in four different shapes. Later, once I have carefully discussed what is remaining in the description of the ark, I shall provide illustrations of these shapes as well as an illustration of the true structure. Here, I have placed a cross-section of the two-part face showing the width and height of the ark, where the line BA signifies the cubit-high peak (Figure 1).

38 *Architecture of Vitruvius*, 8.7. "If in channels, the structure must be as solid as possible, and the bed of the channel must have a fall of not less than half a foot to a length of one hundred."

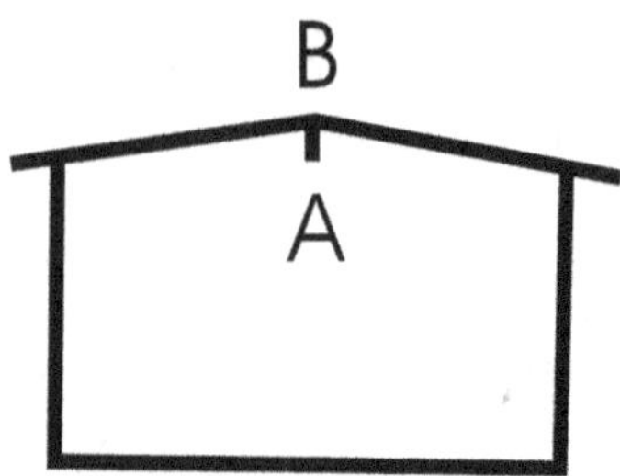

Figure 1. Cross-section of the two-part face showing the width and height of the ark. Line BA signifies the cubit-high peak

7. The door and upper stories

The Vulgate renders the passage, "You shall put the door of the ark on the side below you shall make *coenacula* and a *tristega* in it." If *below* refers to what precedes it, it would be contrary to the sense of the Hebrew. But if it refers to what follows (*i.e.*, *coenacula*), the meaning of the word would appear to be self-contradictory, since *coenaculum* (as Varro testifies[39]) is a place where people dine. But after the practice of eating in an upper story began, the upper story of a house became universally called *coenacula*. Vitruvius also confirms this, writing as follows: "For when it became necessary for the Romans to live in *coenacula* due to overpopulation, they resorted to several-story buildings."[40] And Cicero says concerning an agrarian law, "Rome was built in the mountains, then lifted up and suspended in *coenacula*."[41] Therefore, here it is no less inconsistent to have translated *coenacula* than if you said upper for lower. And the word *tristega* is Greek, the same as *tria tuguria* (three dwellings), which, nevertheless, the translators of the Septuagint do not use, but rather they render it thus: "κατάγαια διώφορα καὶ τριώφορα," that is, "*apothecae* of two floors and three floors." The *apotheca*, however, was actually a lower and larger room where produce and grain were stored for preservation purposes. Both Pliny[42] and Columella[43] have used this meaning frequently. And repositories of this kind suit my proposition

39 *De Lingua Latina*, Chapter 5 §162.

40 *Architecture of Vitruvius*. 2.8. "...so that from the great population of the city innumerable houses would be required. Since, therefore, the area it occupies would not in such case contain the number to be accommodated, it became absolutely necessary to gain in height that which could not be obtained on the plan. ...they obtained in the upper story excellent dining rooms."

41 *De Lege Agraria Oratio Secunda*, 35 §96.

42 *Natural History*, 2.15.6.

43 *On Agriculture*, 1.6.

amazingly well for housing the animals. But lest anyone think that all of the *apothecae* were placed in the lower stories by virtue of the word's meaning, it is added "of two stories and three stories." For as supplies of every kind were brought into the ark by God's command, so it was necessary to store them in various repositories separately and in an organized manner, not only for preservation so they naturally would not get mixed up and spoil, but also for ease of distribution. Some newer translations render it, "you shall make lower and second and third." What, I ask, could be more confusing and senseless than to speak this way using adjectives only and no nouns?

Moreover, when it is said about the position of the door that it was "off the slant," you should understand this as from the right or left side of the length of the Ark, near the sides, which are corners, but not the planes or walls (as it were) by which the Ark was bound together, as many have misunderstood it. This also could be said to be "from the side" or "at the side," but not "off the side" or "on the side," as a number have said. For who has ever seen a door built into a corner? These are generally accepted concerning the provisions of what is written. But, as they contain difficult words with a number of possible meanings, the remaining should be investigated using architectural reasoning and well-reasoned conjecture so that we may seek with all diligence to understand so famous a work more fully.

8. The cubits and the measure thereof

The number of cubits used in the measurements for the ark is agreed upon by tradition, but many debate the actual length of a cubit. Although many say that a cubit is one and one-half feet (which is true), some would add to this another half-foot, even though they cannot substantiate this claim with any actual proof. Quite a few others wish to extend it all the way to nine feet. For yet others, it seems best to estimate the length of the foot and cubit not as we do today, but rather as they were in ancient times when larger bodies were measured with larger units whose exact length is uncertain. Even though in the Holy Scriptures there is frequent mention of cubits, I find their exact length mentioned not more than once, and even this is hardly clear. The place is in the third chapter of Deuteronomy concerning Og the king of Bashan, who alone survived from the race of giants, when his bed is said to have been made of iron and to have been nine cubits in length and four in width, according to the measure of a man's forearm [Deut. 3:11]. The Greek version renders this "ἐν πήχει ἀνδρός," which is "in a man's forearm." The forearm extends from the middle of the elbow joint all the way to the end of the middle finger, never exceeding one and one-half feet in a man who has been formed properly by nature and not deformed. Vitruvius, the most reliable authority in defining measurements, citing a number of Greek authorities, proves the same figure: that one cubit is six hands, and that one foot consists of four hands, and that one hand is four fingers, and that a man is so proportioned that one cubit is one-fourth of his total height, but that one foot is one-sixth of his total height[44]. It is certain however that the Roman system of measurements was derived from the Greek, as were many other good things. And the Greeks used that of the Egyptians, although they did so hiding their sources everywhere. The Hebrews are said to have instructed the Egyptians in these things. Moses himself, who gave us the measurements for the ark, was well versed in all the wisdom of the Hebrews and Egyptians. Also, all the Hebrew Rabbis agree among themselves on the length of these cubits that they are one and one-half feet in length. Of course, when speaking of cubits, feet, hands, fingers, and other such measurements derived from the human body, you could possibly say that they have diminished in length after the Flood: to what extent is uncertain. Furthermore, when our orthodox writers saw the work of the Greatest Workman attacked and brought into disrepute by the slanders of heretics, in refuting them they calculated a cubit length six times greater than I have said, that is, that it was nine feet. And this opinion is now held by all. I have seen nobody that says otherwise, although there are some passages in the Scriptures that would argue against such a measurement. I will now discuss one or two of these. It is said in the book of Kings concerning Goliath the Philistine that his height was six cubits and one hand [I Samuel 17:4]. If you argue that these cubits were nine feet each, Goliath would have been fifty four feet and one hand tall. Therefore his head, according to normal human proportions, would have been about nine feet tall. A normal human frame does not extend to such a height. For how could David have stood before Saul, as it is written, holding the head cut off from Goliath in his hand? In addition to this, when it was commanded in Exodus that an altar be built three cubits in height [Exodus 27:1], these cubits could not possibly be understood to be nine-foot cubits, since that would amount to twenty-seven feet. For this would be useless for making sacrifices unless a ladder had first been put against the altar (which of course would be altogether inappropriate in a holy ceremony). But I will discuss this exaggeration of cubit-length, where this error came from, and how great it is after I have shown the case for the true one-and-one-half-foot cubit by first examining the actual construction of the ark in detail. For another group of heretics, whom St. Augustine recalled in the fifteenth book of *The City of God*, makes light of this way of reckoning with their usual hostility, by foolishly arguing that an ark of such size could not possibly be constructed.[45] I will briefly demonstrate to the contrary using architectural science. I know that the

44 *Architecture of Vitruvius*, 3.1.
45 *City of God*, 15.27.

following section will be somewhat difficult to understand for those who have not been acquainted with literature of this sort.

9. The building of the ark: how it may have been constructed

So I may begin at the bottom and so the explanation of the measurements will be easier, let us say that the base of the ark was 450 feet long (using the one-and-one-half-foot cubit), but 75 feet wide, and 45 feet high (not including the one-cubit peak). It should be pointed out, however, that all these measurements should be understood as internal measurements that do not take into account the thickness of the material. We should carefully consider the strength of the entire superstructure, but most especially that of the base, upon which the weight of the ark and the mass of the entire structure rested. Therefore, I know that no one could possibly deny that such a thing together with its superstructure could have been constructed with this design, unless they were completely ignorant of the science of building. First, 100 one-and-one-half-foot solid squared beams would be placed across the entire width of the bed, equally spaced out. But the two beams forming the ends of the two shorter sides of the base would have to be somewhat thicker than the others. These would be cut to half the thickness at the ends for one and one-half feet and would be firmly held in place by sixteen-inch-thick beams in a double row that would lie across on top. The right and left ends would be left jutting out so the bottoms of one-foot vertical posts and of the two-foot corner posts could be tied into them using a mortise and tenon joint. But the top ends of all these would butt into mortised beams. And the beams would themselves be held in position by four side-braces (twelve feet long and fastened diagonally into the corners) and by iron clamps. The floor of the base would then be constructed on top of the beams to a thickness of eight inches. On the outside, four-inch-thick boards would cover the vertical posts sideways along the perimeter. Inside, however, they would be firmly fastened with clamps and bands. On top of these, seven composite crossbeams, equally spaced out, and the ark's two gable ends would fit against higher beams and firmly support the upper edge of the ark by running along its width. Nevertheless, fourteen solid wooden columns would extend from the bottom and support the crossbeams (two columns to each crossbeam). Two diagonal braces would support each column from either side and together with the support of the other props would hold up the first story at the height of four cubits. Two other stories would follow the first: a middle story eight cubits high, and an upper story ten cubits higher than the middle. Diagonal braces around the columns and other supports perpendicular to the lower beams would support the upper stories. Above the middle of the crossbeams and two gable ends, nine posts one cubit long would hold up the ridgepole of the roof along with the roof supports. Rafters would slope down from these on the left and right and jut out equally past the long sides of the top of the ark. The roofing placed on top of these would cover the structure, and the eaves themselves would keep water from dripping down the side of the ark.

10. The use of the floors

The use of the different floors was as follows: stalls (or if you prefer, kennels) were placed on the first floor for all the quadrupeds and reptiles, suitable for each kind and enclosed with bars and grates. There were walkways arranged along the length and width, so that people could easily see everything and supply anything needed. Also there would have been a need for openings and holes to be left through which droppings could fall into the bottom of the ark as into the bilge. The entire bilge would actually need to be empty to a height of four cubits for this purpose, unless perhaps some ballast were placed there as well (as is necessary for sailing). Between the middle and upper story, storerooms would have contained grain of every sort for the animals below, each of these itself separated into two or three levels – I have given my reasons for this above. There was no need that all of them be made the same size, but only that they be adapted to the needs of the supplies they were storing: hay lofts, chaff houses, some larger than the grain storage to hold leafy branches, and some even larger than these that could hold acorns, nuts, walnuts, and chestnuts. And again wherever feed was being stored, these floors would keep the various kinds separate: such as spring and fall hay (which is called second hay), mixed fodder, vetch, clover, fenugreek, *erui*, and chickling vetch. And in other places where seed crops and legumes were being stored, the kinds would be kept separate by these floors. It would have been most convenient to add paths to the storerooms and holes in these paths, directly above the stalls, so that food for the animals, even for several days, could easily be dropped from above. Water also could be distributed into these with little difficulty through spigots or pipes (which the mechanics call siphons) and channels carrying water into the stalls of all the animals. In the middle part of the top floor there was a large room, where the people lived, lighted by the ark's window, which, being rather large, had shutters, and was equipped with glass to keep out the weather while letting in the daylight. A pantry would have adjoined this room and a kitchen with a stone hearth, hand-mills, and ovens as well. Likewise, there would have been men's and women's quarters, two rooms of course, one for the men and the other for women where they could have privacy. (It is the accepted opinion of scholars that the men on the ark always slept separately from the women.)[46] These other rooms would have had indirect light (as the light-specialists call it) from the main room. But in other places, they would have used lanterns whenever it was necessary. Near the kitchen there was a woodpile of treated logs (which are called *acapna*, that is *without smoke*). And above it was a storage room for charcoal. But the bedrooms would have been arranged in the manner of modern pig-stalls. After these the barn followed and storerooms filled with every kind of farm crop, and then others reserved for bird feed. The enclosures and cages for all the birds were located on this top floor, and an arrangement of paths with small spaces left between the joints so they would be like vents to cool the air – the air would have been hot because of the breathing of the animals below – and provide a source of fresh air. In addition, the upper surface had vents on either side, left by necessity of the construction, as the thickness of the rafters would prevent it being sealed, so the topmost rafters would not be joined to the crossbeams of the upright posts. Regardless, neither light nor any rain water would fall into the ark from here because of the roof's eaves. There would undoubtedly have been ladders placed above in convenient spots to allow easy access to all the upper floor. You should take the distribution of the weight and passengers to be such that the craft would be carried above the waters in a balanced position. The somewhat long shape of the craft, as it was particularly suited for carrying a great weight, so also had a particular need for a proportion of this type.

11. The type of wood used

If someone should argue that the width or height of the ark could not be joined continuously and with a single length of boards because wood cannot be obtained to such a length (as I mentioned before), let him read the histories of the world and he will find that trees of the Hyrcanian forest are amazing beyond belief and that in some islands trees grow to a length of 144 feet. Pliny believed that he saw in Rome the largest tree of his time, which Tiberius Caesar used for a bridge in a mock naval battle.[47] It was the trunk from a larch tree 120 feet long at a thickness of two feet. "It can be inferred from this," said Pliny, "that the remaining height is scarcely believable to those who calculate its very

46 This opinion can be found in the Midrash Rabbah, 31.12. "As soon as Noah entered the Ark, cohabitation was interdicted him; hence it is written, AND THOU SHALT COME INTO THE ARK, THOU, AND THY SONS—apart; AND THY WIFE, AND THY SONS' WIVES—apart." (Trans. Freedman 1939).

47 *Natural History*, 3.16.76.

top."[48] Another tree in Cyprus cut down for Demetrius' unidecireme[49] was reported to have been 130 feet long and as wide as three men standing abreast. But what need is there to go seek out evidence from the distant past, when we frequently see fir trees in our own Dephinatic mountains taller than 80 feet.

12. The position of the door & a description of the stalls

It would not have been convenient to place the door of the ark in the bottom by the bilge, but it would rather have been located so as to have its entrance into the first story where the animals were, and the hinges would have been positioned on the bottom side of the opening so that the door would open out onto the ground and would act as stairs ascending four cubits. Hugo, who has published a treatise on Noah's ark, believes that the door was not near the bottom as I have stated, but was placed higher up in the part of the ship that stood out of the water, so the outside of the door would meet anyone swimming toward the ark on an equal plane.[50] I would agree with this opinion if it were agreed that animals swam up to the ark as the Flood was beginning. But before the beginning of the Flood (as it is written), "men themselves and every animal according to its kind came to Noah into the ark, and the Lord closed the door [Genesis 7:16]." It is also likely that they did not think they would be able to close the door well enough to close its seams against the water. The same author (Hugo), as well as some others, argues that there were stalls, or kennels, not inside the ark, but outside of it, to hold the kind of animal that the Greeks call amphibian.[51] He says this due to the fact that they require not only food from land but also from water, and are not more at home with dry ground than they are with a pond. This type would include geese, gulls, ducks, swans, kingfishers, and some other small birds; but quadrupeds of this type would be the crocodile, the otter, the beaver, and some other smaller animals. These authors do not think that such animals can be kept inside. But this is not true. Animals of this sort can easily tolerate life outside of water, even those that eat fish, as long as they have meat instead of fish. For once while I was in Paris I saw two fish of the type that are called seals, drawn in a cart from a long way away to our kingdom for display. They were no less willing to eat chunks of meat than they were fish. If there was any need of fish for food, it was possible that a water tank was built in the ark, as we read was made in the famous ship of Hiero, king of the Sicilians. In that ship there was a triple deck, equipped with sixty triple-rowing benches, but only twenty rows for rowing. But pertaining

48 ibid.
49 Demetrius' galley of 11 tiers of oars. *Natural History*, 16.76.40.
50 *De Arca Noe Morali*, I.12.
51 ibid.

to our topic, Atheneus writes this: "There was a closed tank of water at the prow, containing 2,000 *metretas*, made from wickerwork, pitch, and linen. Near this there was also a fish pool lined with sheets of lead and wooden planks, full of sea water, where many fish were easily kept alive."[52] Moreover, those that would position kennels for amphibians outside the ark can see themselves how they hold a position against the teaching of the Lord, who commanded, "from all the animals of all flesh you shall take two into the ark to live with you [Genesis 6:19]." And again, "Two from each shall enter with you, so they may live [Genesis 6:20]." And the Scriptures repeat this and what was done afterwards saying, "from every thing that moves upon the earth two and two came to Noah and entered the ark [Genesis 7:15]."

13. Carnivores

The theologians agree unanimously that no carnivore in the ark lived by catching its own food. Because, they say, it would have been breaking God's command to keep animals for the purpose of feeding others in the ark in addition to the number given by God, and that it should rather be believed that there was some kind of food other than meat that could suffice for all. For as Saint Augustine says, many animals that live on meat eat produce and grain, especially figs and chestnuts, and hunger forces living things to eat what is available, and there is nothing good and wholesome that God cannot accomplish.[53] To this I shall just say briefly that the animals numbered for us were those that entered into the ark willingly, just as it is written, so that they could live with Noah and preserve their seed over the face of the whole earth. But the entire command also includes other animals brought along specifically for food. Thus He says, "You shall therefore take with you from all the foods which can be eaten, and you shall carry them with you, and they shall be food for you and them (the animals)." How, therefore, could Noah have obeyed the essential point of the whole command if he left out meat, the sole food of many beasts and birds? Or who would ever believe that lions, wolves, leopards, tigers, species of eagles and hawks, and then every kind of bird with hooked beak and talons could live on fruit, vegetables, and chestnuts for an entire year? Indeed, any talk of food that would suffice for all animals is clearly rubbish. Nor do we doubt anything concerning God's power. But this is a question of what God commanded, not what He is able to do. Therefore Noah himself was the one who saw that meat was brought on board, and he did not sin by adding to the Lord's command, rather he would have been sinning to fail to take meat with him.

52 *The Deipnosophists or Banquet of the Learned of Athenaeus,* Volume I, 5.42.
53 *City of God,* 15.27.

14. The builders and workmen of the ark

Some question how a ship of such enormous size and requiring so much labor could possibly have been constructed by four men (*i.e.*, Noah and his three sons), and over the period of 100 years that the Scriptures say the construction lasted. Let us say to this with Augustine that additional workmen were used for the ark in addition to the four.[54] In large constructions there is indeed not only a need for a lot of labor, but also for a lot of laborers, since many problems arise that a small number of men would be unable to deal with efficiently. It would be absurd to doubt that the builder God chose for His work had the help he needed as well as the necessary skill and the understanding. Without these things any attempt to build the ark would have failed. I would not, however, deny that Noah, acting as the head-builder, together with his sons and some helpers, was able to accomplish the project within 100 years. This would be the same as if he had had 300 builders with attending laborers working for one year. For it is known from Plutarch's histories that King Hiero, once he had brought all the necessary lumber from Mount Aetna, completed the ship I have mentioned above within twelve months. He accomplished this task with 300 skilled workmen in addition to laborers, under the supervision of Archia of Corinth.[55] Therefore, as we have seen what is relevant to the nature of the ark, it now remains that we make the important measurements clear.

15. The capacity of the ark

I have demonstrated here the length of a half-foot with the line BA, which doubled makes up what the Parisians call the Royal Foot and is used in both public and private construction. Therefore, the measurements I am about to use in my geometrical description will be fixed and certain. This same line BA tripled will make the one-and-one-half-foot cubit, which I use as the standard measurement in the description of our ark, to make its length absolutely certain. We shall make a line bc (Figure 2), one cubit of the nature I have just described, and from the line bc the square D shall be drawn. Likewise, from the same line the cube M shall be defined. Therefore the square D will be a square cubit, and the cube M shall be a solid cube, or corporeal cube, which we also call a cubic cubit. To calculate the volume of the ark, that is the total corporeal size, which is its capacity, first find the area of the base (which is also called

54 Homily 373,4.

55 Buteo apparently mistakenly gave Plutarch credit. The reference is *The Deipnosophists or Banquet of the Learned of Athenaeus*, 5.40.

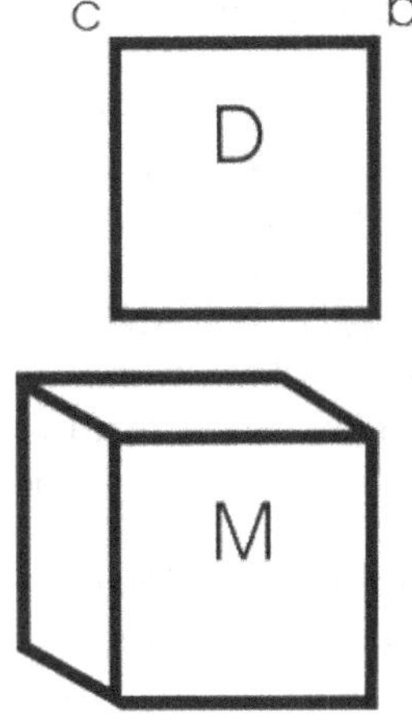

Figure 2. Square D will be a square cubit, and the cube M shall be a solid cube, or corporeal cube, which we also call a cubic cubit.

its quadrature) by multiplying the length (300 cubits) by the width (50 cubits). This is 15,000 square cubits. Multiply this amount again by the height (30 cubits), and you have 450,000 cubic cubits. This is the volume of the inside of the ark to the beginning of the roof. The remaining space to the peak, as it is a triangular prism, contains half of its rectangular parallelepiped (*i.e.*, 7,500 cubits). Add this to the 450,000 cubits, and the total volume for the whole ark is 457,500 cubic cubits. But this space is occupied by various impediments, such as columns and their supports, the thickness of the floors, and the boards forming the stalls and storerooms. Therefore, we will compensate for these by deducting the space of the triangular prism (the roof) from our calculations. Therefore the space remaining in the ark is 450,000 cubic cubits. I will now demonstrate that this space is easily sufficient to contain seed from all the animals.

16. The animals listed by kind

Since I have now discussed the shape of the ark, the nature of its construction, and its size, using architectural and geometric methods, it is no small difficulty that remains in the proposed work to prove how the capacity of this ark was sufficient to hold all of the given kinds of animals on earth and food for each sufficient for a year. For this is what the heretics ridicule most. To deal with this, therefore, I have conducted a careful investigation of those writers who took care to record such things for posterity. I will list below all the kinds of quadrupeds by name[56], distinguishing the clean from the unclean by designating them as seven each or two each. The opinion of those who double those numbers (when they distinguish the two kinds of animals) is widely rejected. And because not everyone has seen all these species of animals or read about them, I shall list them by comparing them to three well-known species: the cow, the sheep, and the wolf. This simplification, of course, will make the matter much easier to comprehend.

56 This list of quadrupeds seems to come mostly from Pliny's *Natural History*, Book 8.

According to Pliny, the largest of all the land animals is the elephant.[57] And according to Aristotle, it is four times as large as the cow.[58] Therefore, I calculate that two elephants would be equivalent to eight cows in terms of space and food required. In the Hercynian forest there are beasts called wild oxen slightly smaller than elephants that have the appearance and color of bulls. Neither Pliny nor any other natural historian mentions them, but Caesar writes about them in his *Commentaries*.[59] And they should not be considered clean animals, because it is known that no wild animal without horns chews cud. We shall then assume that two wild oxen are equivalent to six cows. In the same forest there is a kind of one-horned ox that looks like a horse, which Caesar also mentions in his *Commentaries*.[60] So, for these I shall estimate two cows. There are four kinds of camels: the Arabian (of course), the Bactrian, the so-called dromedary, and the giraffe.[61] These together are four pairs, but equivalent to sixteen cows. Two rhinoceroses would be like four cows. Unicorns, two; bison, two; buffalo, two; European bison, two; oryx, two; reindeer, two; winged horses with horns called *pegasi*, two; one-horned Indian oxen (also with solid hooves), two; ostriches (more of a land animal than a kind of bird, for they only have wings to help them run; otherwise, they are not flying creatures), two; common cows, seven; deer, seven (equivalent however to four cows); antelope (*i.e.*, the goat-stag), seven (equivalent to four cows); red deer, two; common horses, two; wild horses, two; spotted horses, two; hippopotamuses (*i.e.*, river horses), two; donkeys, two; wild donkeys, two; one-horned Indian donkeys, two; bears, two; pigs, two; boars, two. All the animals of this sort eat both forage and grain, either a mixture or each separately. In these, however, there is no need to estimate: they should be considered equal to cows. Although in some cases I may err by estimating too much, in none am I estimating too little. Therefore, all of these together correspond to forty five and one-half pairs of cows. Nevertheless, in case my calculations and those of the men who have investigated such things in antiquity are in some error, I shall leave extra space making the calculation forty five and one-half pairs an even sixty pairs of cows.

---

57 *Natural History,* 8.1.

58 *Historia Animalium,* 2.17. The exact quote is "...its liver is four times as large as the ox's, as are its other internal parts, though its spleen is disproportionately small."

59 *Caesar's Commentaries on the Gallic War,* 6.28.

60 *Commentaries,* 6.26.

61 This may be based on a reading of Pliny (*Natural History,* 2.8.26), who listed the Bactrian and Arabian as the "two kinds" of camels, but then also noted, "Two other kinds of beasts there be, that resemble in some sort, the Camels." (2.8.27) Here Pliny lists only the Camelopard, or giraffe, and Buteo may have inferred the dromedary was the fourth camel omitted by Pliny.

17. The names of the smaller animals that eat both forage and grain

It is said that there are four kinds of sheep and ram, domesticated and wild. And if these are all clean, they make up seven times four, which is twenty-eight sheep. There are also several kinds of goat. For in addition to the domestic goat, there are two undomesticated varieties, the so-called wild goat and the mountain-goat; likewise, there is the incredibly fast ibex, whose head is weighed down by huge horns; there is the oryx, whose fur is turned backwards toward its head; also, there is the gazelle, the addax antelope, and the twisted-horn antelope. It is unlikely, however, that these eight kinds are all clean, because (as I mentioned before) it is known that no wild animal without horns chews cud. Therefore, I have estimated the entire goat family at thirty sheep. The ape family also has a number of varieties, such as the monkey, the cebus, the baboon, the long-tailed monkey, and others of that type. I shall treat them as ten sheep. The hare, two; the Alpine white hare, two; the rabbit of the hare family, two; the common rabbit, two; the wild rabbit, two; badgers (also called *taxo*), two; squirrels, two; dormice, two. There is also the complicated mouse family, which would include moles. (There are those, however, who think that mice were not brought in the ark nor anything of that family since they are born of corruption,[62] as they also say of mules because they come from another kind.) Hedgehogs, two; porcupines, two. We shall estimate all these very small animals (starting with the hare) at four sheep. Therefore the sum of all these animals comes to forty pairs of sheep.

18. The names of those animals that eat meat

The most famous of the carnivorous animals is the wolf. Therefore all the other carnivorous animals will be compared to the wolf. Lions, two; leopards, two; leucrocota (about the size of a donkey), two; *calae*, two; dragons, two; boas, two. I estimate each of these six pairs to be equivalent to four wolves. Thus, the sum is twenty-four wolves. Bulls with flexible horns that live by hunting, two; manticores (particularly fond of eating human corpses), two. For these, I assume the equivalent of twelve wolves. Panthers, two; tigers, two; wolves, two; dog wolves, two; deer wolves (which are also called jackals), two; hellhounds, two; *cephae*, two; lynxes, two; sphinxes, two; hyena, two; wild *axes*, two. Some small animals hunt food in the water but actually live on land. Their names are these: sea otter, beaver, giant otter, satyr, and common otter. The five pairs of this type I make equal to two wolves. The hyena

62 Omission of creatures from the Ark because of a belief in spontaneous generation was common, e.g. Augustine, *City of God*, 15.27 and Hugh of St. Victor, *De Arca Noe Morali*, 1.13. Wilkins (1675, p. 165) is one of the first to omit this detail from his description of animals on the ark.

(that some call the *glavum*), the African hunting dog, the fox, the cat, the Egyptian weasel, the ferret, and the common weasel. For these seven pairs, since they have moderate size, I estimate two wolves. Sea calves (which use fins in the sea, but also use them as feet to crawl on the ground), two. The sum of all these is thirty-two pairs of wolves. But I shall assume some extra so that the total comes to forty pairs of wolves.

19. The distribution of food for the carnivores and the arrangement of the stabling for all, with an illustration

I have calculated that the carnivorous animals were equivalent to forty pairs of wolves. Now, for each pair of wolves I would assign one sheep for every four days for food. Therefore, ten sheep would have been consumed daily for food. By multiplying these by the 365 days in the year, we come to 3,650 sheep for a year's food. Now that this is established, it remains for me to demonstrate how all of the quadrupeds listed above (*i.e.*, 120 cows, 3,730 sheep, and 80 wolves) could be stabled on one story (as I have already said), which was four cubits from the bottom of the ark and eight cubits from the middle story. First, there would have been a hall six cubits wide that ran along the entire length of the ark's side from the door, which I estimate was twenty feet from the corner of the ark. This hall would have ended in a staircase on either end leading to the upper floors. A second hall eight cubits wide, extending to the opposite side of the ark, would have been joined to the middle of the first one at a right angle. This second hall would have run between two sections of rectangular stalls, sixty in number, each five cubits long and three and two-thirds cubits wide. These stalls would have been positioned along either side of the second hall all the way to the first hall. They would have been side by side, except for being separated by two smaller hallways that crossed through the second hall at a right angle, forming a total of six (as it were) divisions, each divided crosswise with stalls. Each pair of cows could be contained within one of these, but it would have been necessary that some be somewhat larger in proportion to the size of the animals. For example, the stall for the two elephants, which were calculated as four pairs of cows, would have occupied the space of four stalls. The forty pairs of various smaller animals (calculated using the size of a sheep) would have been contained in their own three-cubit rectangular stalls, positioned in two rows across the width of the ark up to the first hall. These smaller stalls would have been separated from the larger stalls by two more hallways crossing the middle of the ark, equal in size and parallel to the second hallway. Adjacent to the sheep stalls on either side, there would have been housing for the forty carnivores in stalls three cubits wide but four cubits long. The rows of these stalls would have ended in two hallways four cubits wide to provide easy access for the sheep to be fed to the carnivores. Thus, the space remaining for occupation on the first story on either side of the sheepfolds would have been 228 cubits long and 44 cubits wide. This dimension encloses 10,032 square cubits. If these were allotted for the 3,650 meat-sheep, the space for each comes to slightly less than five and one-half square cubits. It is not, however, out of the question that those sheep brought for food, if it was necessary, could have been stabled in the upper stories of the ark, the bottom, or even some other place. Thus the first story could have contained twice the number of animals and stalls that I have calculated. I have included an illustration of this here (Figure 3).

Figure 3. Floorplan of the first floor.

20. Concerning the food for non-carnivorous animals

I believe I have already sufficiently shown that every kind of quadruped, both for preserving and for meat, could have been kept on one story of the ark with plenty of space. But this is not sufficient for the controversy at hand, unless I have also proven that the food in the storehouses would suffice for the use of an entire year. There are hardly any animals that eat produce that would not prefer grain. Provisions of grain are stored more compactly and are more easily handed than those of produce. I would put it like this: ten pounds of hay or vetch hay occupy more space than ten pounds of barley or vetch grain. Take the amount of hay that can sustain a cow for a day, and the same amount of meal or mash from any grain is more than enough to even fatten a cow for two or three days. But so I may better defend the capacity of the ark from the slanders of its detractors, I shall demonstrate that it would even have been possible in the ark to store enough hay, the most cumbersome feed of all, to keep the animals alive for a year. For in previous chapters I have already converted the bodies of all the larger animals into the equivalent of 60 pairs of cows (120 cows total) and the bodies of the smaller animals kept for preservation into 80 sheep. The number of the other animals which I included for food for the carnivores would have decreased by ten each day, so the amount of food required to support them for a year would also have decreased. And so the given number of the flock (3,650 sheep) does not consume any more in a year than a sustained flock of 1,820. Although the formula for this calculation is not widely known, I have explained it elsewhere in a treatise on logistics.[63] Add the other 80 sheep to these to get a total of 1,900. But let us assume that seven sheep are equivalent to one cow as far as food is concerned to make the following problem easier to solve. Therefore 1,900 sheep equal 271 3/7 cows. Add to this 120 cows and the sum is 391 3/7. But just to be liberal in my estimate, I shall assume that there were equivalent to 400 cows in the ark that needed to be fed with meadow hay alone for the entire duration of the Flood. Furthermore, while researching the amount of daily food necessary for a cow, I discovered by experimentation that the most reliable authority is Columella, the most learned writer on agriculture. He says that in January thirty pounds of hay is enough for one cow's daily food, but in March and April, because the ground is plowed up, each needs to be given forty pounds.[64] Now it is certain that the pound Columella used was the twelve-ounce pound. Therefore forty of those pounds would now make thirty of the sixteen-ounce pounds that we use today. I have carefully measured compressed hay, such as is typical in large hay-lofts after it has dried, and have found that the size of a solid cubit contains slightly more than forty pounds of hay. Therefore one square bale of hay (I mean here a bale of one cubic cubit) would be more than sufficient to be distributed to each head of cattle daily. In fact, if they were on this diet for long, they would become excessively fat. For (as Aristotle says) all animals, and especially those who have hot stomachs, fatten up with too much rest and lack of exercise.[65] Therefore I have no doubt that half a bale of hay per day would be sufficient for inactive cows. That would be twenty pounds of hay. But so I may stop the mouths of the contentious, I shall calculate one bale of hay given to each cow daily. Therefore 400 cows eating as many bales of hay daily in the space of one year would eat 146,000 bales. I have already arranged it so that the middle story of the ark is ten cubits from the top story, where I placed the storerooms for feed and produce of every kind. But now let us assume that all the space in the ark between these two floors was

63 Though Buteo seems to cite *Logistica*, that work was not published until 1559, five years after *Opera Geometrica*. Buteo may refer to an earlier manuscript version of *Logistica* or an unpublished work.

64 *On Agriculture*, 6.3.4-6.

65 *Historia Animalium*, I.3.17. The exact quote is "Most animals grow fat round the belly, and especially those animals which do not move about much."

filled with meadow hay. Therefore, since the length of this hayloft would be 300 cubits, the width 50 cubits, and the height 10 cubits, the total space would come to 150,000 cubic cubits, which exceeds the annual consumption of hay for 400 cows by 4,000 cubic cubits. From this we can see that this middle story is not only enough but excessive for the food for the quadrupeds, even if there were twice as many. Among these I placed the larger reptiles, such as pythons, crocodiles, hippopotamuses, sea calves, and boas. Nature has made the others small of body, such as vipers, serpents, asps, horned snakes, hydras, basilisks, lizards otherwise green and tiny, geckos, chameleons, salamanders (who are so tough that they can put out fires by the touch just like ice).[66] These, however, and any others of this sort could easily live in small holes made around the stabling area and wood. It should be thought that every kind of dog lived in the kitchen where they could find food. No animal vomits its filth and eats it again more frequently than the dog. And its pernicious rabies is a nuisance both to itself and others. Therefore, it seems that dogs in the ark were a prototype of heretics.

21. The third floor

Now on the highest floor I have placed lodging for people and all the birds (although without enumerating them or distinguishing their kinds), along with storerooms and necessary food, throughout distinct compartments and dividing hallways, just as I arranged the stabling for the quadrupeds. Of course I do not need to explain this arrangement here in this section. But rather I should give the reasons why a place of such magnitude would be constrained by such restrictive arrangements. For although birds are varied and are almost as diverse as quadrupeds, they are so different both in physical appearance, diet, and where they live, that they can hardly be said (even by the most conservative estimate) to be a fiftieth part of the creatures that walk the Earth. But since the first floor housed all the quadrupeds as well as their fodder, the bipeds (which are left) should have been placed in the rest of the ark. Although, it is not unbelievable that Noah himself had foreknowledge of the future (*i.e.*, that all things would be undone in the cataclysm) and had stowed aboard plenty of equipment, agricultural and urban, and every kind of workman's tool in empty spaces in the ark. If indeed it was necessary that fish be kept in the ark for feeding the amphibians and the fish-eating birds, a fish tank could have been built in this part in the manner described above. And it could have been easily filled using a Ctesibian machine or some other sort of water pump and drained again by pulling the piston out through the cylinder. Now in the course of our discussion I think I have come to the point where no further objections

66 *Natural History*, 2.10.67

can be made that an ark composed of one-and-one-half-foot cubits would not have been large enough to save all of animal kind from the Flood. I have included a sketch here to illustrate this discussion (Figure 4).

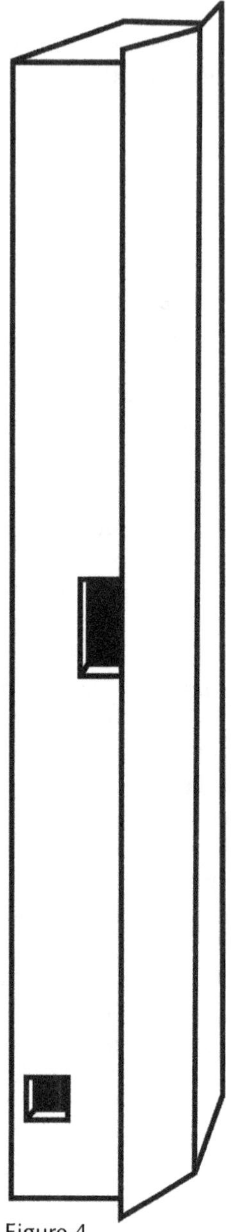
Figure 4.

22. The nine-foot cubit, and how this error came about

It will not be enough, perhaps, to have proved at length and with many arguments that cubits were one and one-half feet long, unless I also refute the cubit that is six times larger (*i.e.*, the nine-foot cubit now long accepted in the view of most scholars). I find that this error has been caused by a poorly understood explanation of Origen's. For he speaks along these lines in his second homily on the construction of the ark:

> Some men object to all these built with such skill, and especially Appelles, who was a disciple of Marcion but the inventor of another heresy greater than what he learned from his teacher. Because he, therefore, desired to assign no divine wisdom to the writings of Moses in and of themselves, arguing that they contained no work of the Holy Spirit, he exaggerated sayings of this kind. He also says that it was not possible that such a small space could have contained so many kinds of animals and enough food for them for a whole year. "How," he says, "could such a space as is written have existed? And even so, that space could only have contained four elephants." Then later he adds: "Therefore it is clear that this story is false. And if this story is false, then it is clear that this scripture is not from God."[67] But in response to these

67 This quote in Origen's *Genesis Homily,* II:2 is from Appelles' (more commonly spelled Apelles) *Syllogisms*. This work is not extant. Apelles' work is only known through those who quoted his work.

> objections, we would bring to the notice of our readers what we have learned from wise men who were knowledgeable in Hebrew tradition and from teachers of old. Now the ancients said, Moses, who (as the Scriptures testify about him) was "instructed in all the wisdom of the Egyptians" [Acts 7:22], recorded the number of cubits in this passage in accordance with the science of geometry (in which the Egyptians were especially skilled)." And among geometricians, according to the principle known to them as *virtue*, one square and solid cubit is valued at either 6 cubits (if considered generally) or 300 cubits (if divided up piecemeal). If this reasoning should be employed in the measurement of the ark, such great distances of length and width would be found as would certainly have been able to contain dormant seeds from the whole world and seed to be revived from every living animal. These are what have been said, as far as the historical account is concerned, in response to those who strive to attack the Scriptures of the Old Testament for containing things that are both impossible and irrational.[68]

This is verbatim as a Latin translator has rendered it, since Origen's original Greek does not exist. But St. Augustine, a man famous for his knowledge of holy writings, in his book *On Questions in Genesis* approaches this passage in the following way: "Origen," he says, "solves this question with the geometric cubit, asserting that the Scripture did not speak in vain, because Moses was instructed in all the wisdom of the Egyptians who loved geometry."[69] Then he goes on to say that the geometric cubit was equal to six of the measure of our cubit. If therefore we should understand cubits of this size, there is no question that the Ark was large enough to contain all those things. This is what Augustine said, and every author I have read on the subject follows his authority, because it is deservedly great. I held the same opinion myself until I looked into the matter more closely and geometry herself showed me the truth. But as for those who have no knowledge of geometry, it is not strange that they err on this point, since the subject is hardly a matter of common sense. For if from this passage of Origen you wish to simply extend the length of the cubit to six, I could just as easily extend it to 300, since the author speaks about either (although no one has been so audacious as to claim the latter). By extending this cubit like this, the matter would be concluded so that the same cubit is both of a larger and smaller size—which is absurd. Therefore we must see in what sense this statement could be true by either measurement. Now I have shown

68 *Genesis Homily,* II.2.

69 *City of God,* 15.27 not *Questions in Genesis* as indicated by Buteo.

in the preceding pages that the volume of the ark contained 450,000 cubic cubits. Therefore the base of the ark can be divided into six equal squares, each with a side of fifty cubits. By squaring that side, you will get 2,500 square cubits (*i.e.*, the surface area of one of the six squares in the base). Again by multiplying the 2,500 cubits of the square by 30 cubits in height, there will be 75,000 cubic cubits. This makes up one sixth of the body of the ark. Therefore, as Origen says, each of these cubits is valued as 6. Because 6 times 75,000 cubic cubits comes to a total of 450,000. This is the capacity of the Ark, the same that I found before in my own calculations. I will now demonstrate the other part of this proposition (*i.e.*, that one cubit can be valued as 300), as follows: Take each of the smaller planes of the ark, one with a side of 30 cubits, the other with a side of 50. By multiplying these two sides together, it comes to 1,500 square cubits. By multiplying this number again with the third dimension of the Ark, you make 300 cubes from each square cubit separately, and in total you make 450,000. But this is the volume of the ark just as has been demonstrated above. And thus according to geometric reasoning, from the cube and the square, what Origen said was correct by either measurement. And this is not because the geometric cubit is equivalent to six of our cubits, as Augustine asserts. Origen did not solve this problem using a geometric cubit, but rather by geometric cubing, since geometricians do not treat cubits different from common usage, but rather cubing. This method of multiplying cubits also works with the prism, the pyramid, and in general for any object for which an equal solid parallelepiped can be made upon a base, which is similar to what the ark had. Yet it should be noted in this statement of Origen's that its chief shortcoming is that the matter, which was already difficult in and of itself because of its technical nature, is made so confusing with his use of enigmatical and convoluted words, that it becomes necessary to guess at them, rather than interpret them. Indeed, it would have been clearer and more natural to say that the numbers of cubits found in the description of the Ark would be found by geometric calculation to make a volume of 450,000 cubits in the Ark. Besides, such an exaggeration of cubits to nine feet (which is widely accepted) removes doubt from those who do not understand geometry, but it implies an enormous and absurd size for the ark for those who do understand it. I have already demonstrated above that the size of the ark (calculated using the one-and-one-half-foot measurement for the cubit) was sufficient to preserve every kind of animal and to store provisions for a year with room to spare. If, however, the ark is supposed to have been in a similar shape to what I described above but measured in nine-foot cubits, it would have been six times longer, wider, and higher than the other, but in volume 216 times larger, seeing that the ratio of like volumes is the cube of the sides. Indeed, if anyone does not get these results with the rudiments of geometry, he will find them by this calculation: because a nine-foot cubit contains in it six one-and-one-half-foot cubits, the length of the larger ark will be 1,800 one-and-one-half-foot cubits, the width 300, and the height 180. When these numbers are multiplied with each other, just as was done before by cubing, you will get the sum 97,200,000 (*i.e.* ninety-seven million, two hundred thousand cubic cubits), which is the volume of the larger ark. By dividing this into the cubes of the other smaller ark (450,000), you will see that it is contained in the larger as many times as I said before. Therefore the ark according to the nine-foot cubit would be 215 times greater than is necessary. So more than the equivalent space of an entire ark of the smaller calculation could be assigned to each pair of cows—nothing is more absurd than this. I would add to this that, if you accept such gigantic cubits, the whole thing begins to verge on fantasy. For it seems to me that a ship of such vast size and carrying such a weight could never be constructed by human power. For (as Vitruvius says) everything cannot be done using the same methods,[70] and in building anything there are limits to how much one can extend measurements, since structures collapse if they are enlarged too much, or else they are too large to be built at all. Therefore, after carefully considering this matter of the six-fold-cubit (founded on no reason at all), who would not now see that it undermines our argument rather than supports it? Concerning this, even Augustine seemed not to be entirely sure. In the 15th book of *The City of God*, when he tries to bring another solution to this question, he says this:

> As for those who say that the size of that ark was not able to contain so many kinds of animals, it seems to me that they take nothing into account except for the length of 300 cubits, and the width of 50, and the height of 30. They forget that there was as much space again in the upper story and that much space yet again in the third, and by this reckoning, that three times the calculated cubits would be 900 long, 150 wide, 90 high.[71]

Augustine infers nothing from this other than that there were three levels in the Ark, parallel to the base, just as I arranged it before. These levels would make three individual arks, as it were, by their own

70 *Architecture of Vitruvius,* 10.22. "For the same principles do not answer in all cases. In some machines the principles are of equal effect on a large and on a small scale; others cannot be judged of by models. Some there are whose effects in models seem to approach the truth, but vanish when executed on a larger scale, as we have just seen. With an auger, a hole of half an inch, of an inch, or even an inch and a half, may be easily bored; but by the same instrument it would be impossible to bore one of a palm in diameter; and no one would think of attempting in this way to bore one of half a foot, or larger."

71 *City of God,* 15.27.

division. And thus the length of the Ark is tripled. But in Augustine's opinion, the width and length would also be tripled. This is entirely false. For thus the parts of something would be greater than its whole, which is impossible. Nevertheless, some actually make an argument from this passage for a laughable calculation of volume by measuring lines alone. But this is no more true than it is that nothing more is required to understand the meaning of words beyond the lines of the characters. But the perversity of heretics has always been such that they mock most what they do not understand. They do not yield to any rational argument, but rather slander those with whom they disagree about the truth. (I have experienced this in certain men who on occasion have debated with me on this question.) For there is hardly any kind of error once condemned and booed off stage that will not be called back to the forefront by some group or the other. And what heretics lack in cleverness for making new arguments they make up for in stubbornness for bringing out old ones. Different elements from these seem right to different heretics, but no one thing seems right to all of them. For wickedness can never get along with itself. These lies about cubits have been spread with craft. But it requires no craft at all to answer the objections of so untaught a mocker. For what need does a blind man have for a mirror? Or a jackdaw for a lyre? (So the old proverb goes.) Thus I am now pleased to go unarmed to meet with the enemy, even were he crowded round by his elephants. What do you say, Marcionita?[72] What do you snarl against the ark of the Lord, heretic? No, rather you trumpet along with your elephants, not African or Indian, but ones so monstrous that you would have four of them fill your ark. Your beasts do not make the ark small, but the ark makes your beasts enormous and renders your whole beast scheme more fantastic than the Trojan horse. For if it could not contain even only four elephants (as you exaggerate), you fabricate a height of more than thirty individual cubits, a length twice as much, with a width of more than twelve cubits. Here you err not so much in your monstrous size as you do with deformity, as the shape would be closer to that of dragons than to elephants. Even if you were to arrange them the other way, the height would remain the same as was given before, with one sixth the former length, and the width of each elephant would fill a quarter of the ark's length. I can find nothing similar to a monster of this kind. Therefore, it is established (as I will conclude with your words against you) that the fictitious account is not the one of the ark's capacity but of your stabling. It is, therefore, what you deny and what the matter itself proves: the writings of this prophet are from God, but yours (as you show) are from your father Satan, who

72 Marcionita refers to Apelles (op cit. 40). Apelles was a follower of Marcion, the second century heretic who rejected the Old Testament God as being a vindictive lover of war. According to his teachings, Jesus Christ was from a higher God than the God of Creation. Marcion taught that only those who followed his teaching would be saved. (Irenaeus, *Against Heresies,* 1.27).

has begotten you and those like you. But now let us leave this fault-finder[73] who makes up monsters for himself. And in addition to the shape of the construction that I have explained in the preceding pages, let us now examine what kind of shapes others have proposed.

23. The various figures of the ark, and their illustrations

All learned interpreters of Moses' description understand the same base, *i.e.*, the shape of a rectangle (as I said before), with one side six times as long as the other. But scholars generally build on the superstructure of the foundation in four different ways. For Origen, in his aforementioned homily, says, "I think that the ark, as much as is clear from the things that are described, had four angles rising from the bottom that gradually narrowed as they came to the peak and came together in the space of one cubit. Thus the cubit is the length and width of the peak."[74] This description of the author would be nothing other than a pyramid with its point cut off, except for the fact that the area of a section was not a square but six times longer than it was wide. Furthermore, a good many others agree with Hugo and put the middle of the Ark at fifteen cubits high on its base, completing the remainder (another fifteen cubits) with a pyramid-shaped roof, also with its point cut off, just like Origen's.[75] But others have rejected the idea that the height was shortened in this way and have proposed a pyramid-shaped roof over the entire structure of the ark (built thirty cubits tall). Yet there is no agreement as to the height of this arched roof. But lately some more recent authors, such as Caietanus, have imagined that the Ark's hull had the shape that geometricians call a prism, in which two parallel planes from opposite sides, resting on the shorter sides of the Ark's base, make up three-sided figures with their vertices cut off to a width of one cubit, but the remaining three planes form a parallelogram.[76] There are a number of problems that argue against shapes of this kind, besides the fact that they do not correspond fully to the arrangement of the prophet. First of all, what do Origen's pseudopyramid and Caietanus' prism have in common with the ark? Then, a square formation of the peak, or rather deformity of the peak, is not only ugly in appearance, but also useless to the ark. You could give no argument in support for the utility of such a shape. Furthermore, the whole pyramid itself would require such an awkward and difficult manner of construction and would be the most ridiculous possible shape for stabling animals. Indeed, such a thing is unthinkable. But even a basic understanding of ships is sufficient to show that these shapes would be

73 Latin *Momos*, god of satire, mockery, censure, spirit of evil spirited blame and unfair criticism.

74 *Genesis Homily*, II.1.

75 *De Arca Noe Morali*, I.3.

76 *Commentary on Genesis*, 6.43

useless for sailing. In ships, the part which is narrowed always slopes down to the keel and is under water, but the greatest width extends out into the open and floats above the water. Therefore the pyramid and the prism would be completely submerged unless they were positioned upside-down so that their peaks were below and the base floated upon nothing above. Furthermore in a pyramid, there would only be a third rather than the whole of the volume that I have demonstrated above to be necessary; and in a prism, there would be a little more than half. Even so, this first shape which is so absurd has several supporters (one of whom was the one whose interpretation is called interlinear), who use an entirely frivolous and preposterous argument. Origen uses this argument to commend his own design when he says, "Considering how much rain was needed for the Flood, no shape could have been given to the Ark more convenient and appropriate than the pyramid, as it would have deflected the torrent of the rainstorms from the top, just as from a roof with its peak brought to a narrow point."[77] I have already disproved this sufficiently from the beginning, where it was established that a cubit-long peak was sufficient for the roof. But see how, while those men tremble at the drops of rain, they submerge themselves in deep waves. But as to the third figure, in which Hugo proposes a chest for half of the ark and a vaulted roof for the other half, this is nothing other than to mix error with the truth.[78] The result is that what was good is corrupted by company with the bad. While the pyramid shape (as I said before) would require a complicated and difficult construction even on a solid base, it would be far more of a trouble and a nuisance and even more undesirable to build it on half the ark. For at the place where two dissimilar shapes join together and press against each other, unless it is very firmly held together by strong joints, numerous crossbeams, and supports for the buttresses, then the lower part will be thrust out by the weight and entire pressure of the roof. And connectors of this kind would be much more of a burden and hindrance to the vessel than a good part of its cargo. Besides the fact that it ruins the quality of the construction, such a mixing of shapes reduces the size of the ark by nearly a third. Indeed, as he is recapitulating his main points, Hugo, who is not otherwise particularly ignorant of geometry, inquires into this very issue and wearies into this very issue and wearies himself at length and to no purpose, ranting about three-sided shapes, perpendiculars, hypotenuses, diameters, and four-sided shapes. And when he is unable to untangle himself from this problem or find a convenient out, he concludes his discussion as follows: "In regard to these three- and four-sided shapes," he says, "there are a number of other geometrical subtleties, all of which we will avoid since they are tedious."[79] But it is clear that he ends this discussion not

77 *Genesis Homily,* II.1.

78 *De Arca Noe Morali,* I.12.

79 *De Arca Noe Morali,* I.3 in *Patrologia Latina.*

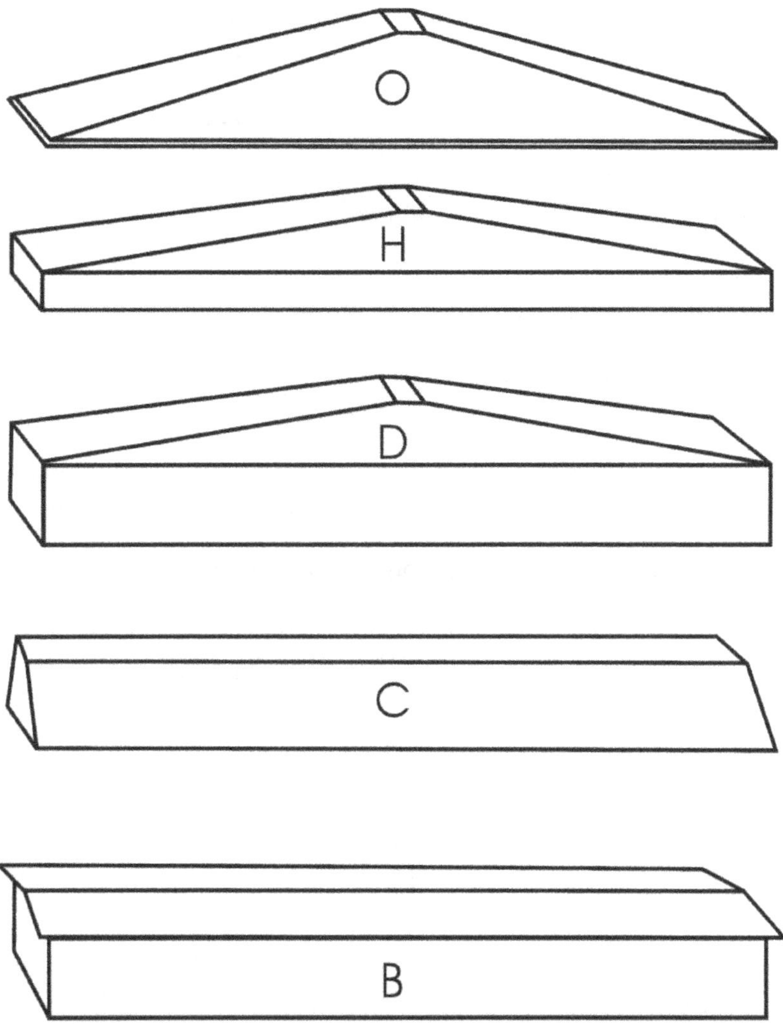

Figure 5.

O. The shape of the ark according to Origen.
H. According to Hugo.
D. According to some scholars.[80]
C. According to Caietanus.
B. According to Buteo.

80 Kircher (1675, p. 43) attributes this shape to Nicholas of Lyra.

so much because it is tedious as because he is incompetent. First, he makes an embarrassing error in his calculations when he says that the diameter (which he calls the diagonal) of the Ark's base was 304 1/4 cubits long.[81] This is not so, because the actual diameter with a square of 92,500 would be shorter than 304 1/4 cubits. So, except that Hugo does not actually show us the inside of his ark, it would be no surprise if he stubbed his toe on the very doorway. Finally, in the fourth structure, the ark derives its shape from God's instructions, and it is truly an 'ark' except for its roof, which, in addition to the other defects I have already mentioned, its creator makes ill-proportioned as a result of impudence as much as from some mistake. But I have included here diagrams of the four shapes I mentioned above, and have also added my own. I believe I have now said enough on this subject, proven my own understanding of the ark, and refuted the objections of the heretics. If by chance while pointing out the errors of others I have made my own (since I am but human), I am not stubborn in asserting them, but completely submit myself to the judgment of the orthodox. Indeed, may it be far from me, that, in examining the physical ark of the Lord to the best of my ability, I should desire to imagine an ark different from the one of which it was only the type, that is, from the Holy Catholic Church. And here let our commentary have its end.

81 *De Arca Noe Morali,* I.3 in *Patrologia Latina.*

IOAN. BUTEONIS

DE ARCA NOË, CUIUS FORMAE, CAPACITATISQUE FUERIT, LIBELLUS.

I. Prooemium

IN ARCAM illam animale seminarium mundi cataclysmo pereuntis iussu Dei fabricata architecto Noë, & a Mose propheta literis proditam, qualis, & quanta fuerit, varie disputatur a multis: Ita ut nec operis forma, neque capacitas inter omnes una conveniat, aliis alio finitionis verba trahentibus, plana quidem ex se satis, & aperta. Sed inest rebus ipsis obscuritas, mistura quadam geometrica prouenient, quae recta etiam sectantibus negocium facessit, haereticis vero caliginem prorsus offundit: ut in opere tanto nihil praeter angustias, quas accusent, videant. Quorum vecordiam catholicorum multi refellentes, rem sane, sicut est, veram credendo, magis quam intelligendo, in eam partem fere peccant, quae periculo vacat. Ut qui laxitate nimia opus extendant, prout validissimis argumentis, hoc est geometricis ostendam. Quae quidem (ut verissime Cicero testatur) non persuadent, sed cogunt. Hoc igitur veniam subsidio nostris, ut aliter instructos arte magis, & virtute, quam numero resistere monstrem. Sic enim & pugnare fortius, & vincere potius erit.

II. Arcae Descriptio Secundum Interpretes.

IMPRIMIS itaque caelestem dominum symmetrias operis praefecto suo praescribentem audiamus. Fac tibi (inquit) arcam de lignis levigatis, mansiunculas in arca facies, & bitumine linies intrinsecus, & extrinsecus. Et sic facies eam: Trecentorum cubitorum erit longitudo arcae, quinquaginta cubitorum latitudo, & triginta cubitorum alti-/6/tudo illius. Fenestra in arca facies, & in cubito consummabis summitatem eius. Ostium autem arcae pones ex latere, deorsum coenacula, & tristega facies in ea. Et quae sequuntur reliqua. Haec est interpretatio vulgata. Septuaginta autem interpretes Graece sic. ποιήσεις οὖν σεαυτῶ κιβωτὸν ἐκ ξύλων τετραγώνων. νοσσιὰς ποιήσεις κατ᾽ τὴν κιβωτὸν, καὶ ἀσφαλτώσεις αὐτωὴν ἔσωθεν, καὶ ἔξωθεν τῇ ἀσφάλτῳ, καὶ οὕτω ποιήσεις τὴν κιβωτόν. τριακοσίων πήχεων τὸ μῆκος τῆς κιβωτοῦ, καὶ πεντήκοντα πήχεων τὸ πλάτος, καὶ τριάκοντα πήχεων τὸ ὕψος αὐτῆς. θυείδα ποιήσεις κατ' τὴν κιβωτὸν, καὶ εἰς πῆχεων συντελέσεις αὐτὴν ἄνωθεν, τὴν δέ θύραν τῆς κιβωτοῦ ποιήσεις ἐκ πλαγίων. κατάγαια διώφορα καὶ τριώφορα ποιήσεις κατ' αὐτήν. Hoc ego Latine sic ad verbum interpretor. Facies igitur arcam ipse tibi ex lignis quadratis. Nidos facies in arca, & bituminabis eam intus & extra, bitumine, & ita facies arcam. Trecentorum cubitorum erit longitudo arcae, & quinquaginta cubitorum latitudo, & triginta cubitorum altitudo ipsius. Fenestram facies in arca, & in cubito perficies eam desuper. Ipsum autem ostium arcae ex obliquo facies. Apothecas duorum tabulatorum, & trium tabulatorum facies in ea. Et ita se habent finitionis praecepta, quorum sensum recentiores aliquot ad Hebraicam (ut ipsi dicunt) veritatem referentes, aliis atque aliis verbis protulerunt, de quibus in expositione sequenti, quoties videbitur locus, mentionem habebo.

III. Explicatio, & Applicatio Verborum Finitionis Ad Opus.

IN ipso statim descriptionis principio sane luculenter per arcam proprium operi nomen assignatur & forma, quo nihil explicatius dari potuit unquam. Est enim arca res humanis usibus frequens, vulgoque notissima. Hac includuntur quae celari, servarique volumus. Unde Varro putat arcam dici, quod ab ea clausa fures arceantur. Et quamvis arcae diversa magnitudine fiant, secundum quod rebus diversis adhibentur (aliae enim sunt vestiariae, aliae nummariae, aliae frumentariae) in omnibus tamen eadem forma fervatur, nisi quod operculo dissimili variantur in summo: quod aut planum est, a fundo distans aequabiliter undique aut incurvum, quod proprie cameratum dicitur, ut in grandioribus, quas indie vocat Iureconsultus Ulpianus cameratas. Et in minoribus etiam, quales mulis clitellariis vectantur frequenter. Aliquae vero sicut frumentariae, quas pro granariis habent pauperes, fastigiato cacuminantur operculo. Caeterum reliqua forma corporis in omni genere conveniunt, quod in longum, latum, atque profundum quinque planis compingitur angulo normali, qui dicitur rectus. Et haec species parallelepipedon rectangulum vocatur in arte. Ad cuius similitudinem arcam etiam illam foederis factam, nullus unquam puto dubitavit, quamvis in descriptione figura non aliter explicetur, quam arcae vocabulo, quod in omnibus scripturae locis Hebraice sonat Aron, haec autem nostra semper Teva, quas voces pro eodem Hebraei ma-/7/gistri semper exponunt. Et interpretes septuaginta pro Aron, & Teua nullo discrimine vertunt κιβωτὸν, & arcam nostri. Est autem expeditum, atque certissimum qualemcunque formam designare eius comparatione rei, quae non aliter atque est, intelligi possit. Quod & Vitruvius cum alias saepe, tum in machinis hydraulicis usurpat, arcam iubens ex aere fabricari: neque rem alioqui difficilem homo vocibus artis instructissimus aliter explicat, quam ipsa nominis proprietate certissima. Cum autem huiusmodi similitudo non habetur in promptu, alias explicatur forma vocibus artis. Sicut in Exodo ubi describitur altare quod habeat quinque cubitos in longitudine, & totidem in latitudine, statim adiicitur, id est quadrum. Sed magis proprie versio Graeca sic, τετράγωνον ἔσαι τὸ θυσιαστήριον: hoc est, quadratum erit altare. Nam nisi quadrati meminisset, poterat intelligi rhombi figura. Quae quidem est laterum quatuor aequalium, non autem rectangula, prout definitur in elementis. His igitur aperte constat, non aliam huic operi formam posse constitui, salvo sensu verborum, & nomine dato, quam quae iam dicta est corporis parallelepipedi rectanguli, cuius longitudo secundum commodulationem symmetriarum positam sit ad latitudinem sexcupla, ad altitudinem vero decupla. Quod tamen errantes nonnulli fecerunt, sicut ad finem voluminis ostendam.

IV. De Arcae Materia.

POST datam formam, materia recte sequitur: quam ex lignis gopher, Hebraeus fermo constituit. Sed quidnam debeat intelligi gopher, interpretes Iudaei, quos ipsorum lingua dicimus Rabinos, tanta confusione disserunt, ut nihil inde stabile finiatur. Alii siquidem pinum, alii abietem, cupressum alii, quidam cedrum esse suspicantur. Thalmudistae quoque cedri genera quatuor faciunt. In eo tamen convenit omnibus, quod unum aliquod arboris genus gopher, accipi censeant. Parum quidem (ut ego puto) verisimiliter, cum vix fieri possit ut una regio materiationem generis eiusdem ea copia suppeditet, quae sufficiat operi tanto: nec unum praeterea genus aliis atque aliis arcae partibus commode satis adhiberetur. Multum nanque distant arbores inter se qualitate. Sunt enim quae trabibus longissimis rigorem fortissime servant, quod basi convenit praecipue. Quaedam vero temperatura leviori comparatae usum tectis egregie praestant. Aliae porro contignationibus, assamentisque tabulatorum sunt praecipuae. Nonnullae ad intestinum opus parvaque secamenta tractabili commoditate probantur. Sed hunc locum interpretes Septuaginta (ut iam supra retuli) verterunt ex lignis quadratis: Noster autem de lignis levigatis transtulit. Quod ad idem ferme recidit. Cum enim tigna dolantur in quadrum, levigata quidem dici possunt, sed neque tam proprie, neque tam intelligenter quam quadrata. Quae quidem deformatio fabricationi nostrae mire congruit, immo necessaria prorsus. Neque enim video quemadmodum /8/ tantae molis aedificium navigationi, vecturaeque sufficiat, nisi totum praeter interiora membra trabibus, tignisque quadratis quam creberrime dispositis, colligationibusque compactis inter se firmissime construatur. Multum etiam firmamenti ad tignorum quadraturam illitum bitumen addebat.

V. De Natura Bituminis.

EST autem natura bituminis (authore Plinio) vicina sulphureae, alibi limus, alibi terra. Limus a Iudeae lacu emergens, cui nomen Asphaltites, ab asphalto voce Graeca bituminis, praeter quod nihil aliud gignit. Terra in Syria circa Sydonem oppidum maritimum. Spissantur haec utraque & in glebas densitate coeunt. Item Ioppe in Syria (teste Vitruvio) Arabiaque Numidarum lacus sunt immani magnitudine, qui emittunt bituminis maximas moles. Et ibi crebrae sunt lapidicinae bituminis duri. Gignitur & pingue, liquorisque oleacei in Sicilia, Acragantino fonte inficiens rivum, eoque utuntur incolae ad lucernarum lumina, olei vice, in reliquo usu aeramentis illinitur, firmatque, ea contra ignes. Placet & in ferrariis fabrorum officinis tingendo ferro, clavorumque capitibus. Ad haec incorrupta vis bitumini aquisque contumax. Ideoque ligna consuerat ne combibant humorem noxium, neque patitur cariem penetrare, tineas, teredinem, termitemque prohibet, propter quae diuturnitatem operibus maxime praestat. Sed & virtus in eo praecipua copulandi praeter materiem etiam corpora. Colligat enim vulnera, nervosque glutinat. Calcis quoque praebuit usum Semiramidi reginae ita ferruminatis latere testaceo Babyloniis muris. Propter has itaque tam opportunas operi nostro virtutes existimo, praeter tignorum frontes intus, & extra, tota quoque latera iuncturarum, dum inter se committerentur, & denique totum opus intestinum linita bitumine. Quod non solum ad coagmenta valuit, sed etiam ad seculi durationem ante cataclysmum, quo tenuit fabrica. Post quem etiam (ut prodit Iosephus) in Cordieo Armeniae monte ubi sidentibus aquis navigium consederat, quaedam reliquiae ad ipsius historici tempora perdurabant, & egressorii nomen a re ipsa, hoc est ab egressu Noe loco remansit. A diluvio autem ad Iosephum supputatione etiam minima tempus annorum plusquam trium millium invenies.

VI. De Arcae Fenestra.

QUOD autem dicitur, Fenestram in arca facies, non ex abundanti videtur hîc arcae mentio repetita: sed eo respectu, ne quis forte putaret ipsam fenestram in tecto collocari: ut errantes quidam opinati sunt, sicut nunc passim in domorum tegulis est videre. Tectum enim habuit arca necessario propter pluvium caeli statum diebus totis quadraginta continuum. Quod etiam ex subiectis liquido patet ubi dicitur, Aperiens Noe tectum arcae. Ceterum inter Rabinos non /9/ nulli volunt hic esse fenestram nihil aliud quam lucernam ex gemma grandiori, ut pote lichnite, seu carbunculo, quae radiantis fulgore lapidis aedificium totum illuminaret. Quorum impudens mendacium arguit aperte quod statim scribitur: Aperiens Noe fenestram quam fecerat dimisit corvum. Alii autem fieri non posse videntes, ut ad tantam amplitudinem corporis uniuersi, membrorumque separatim unius aperturae lumen sufficeret, fenestras pluribus locis in arca positas opinantur. Istam autem omnium fuisse maxima, & ideo solam in praecepto poni.

Hanc opinionem nostrorum multi referentes disquisitione nulla relinquunt in medio. At ego dico, nihil omnino fuisse necessarium arcam fieri luminosam, nisi tantum in ea parte quae fuit hominibus habitatio, quaequidem communi doctorum sententia summum in arca tenebat videmus enim feras animantes, atque reptilium genus omne tenebras non solum nihil abhorrere, vel refugere, sed institutione quadam naturali semper appetere, in hisque morari, nisi dum ventris necessitas cogit ad pastum. Aliae quidem foveas non uno loco sibi cavant, quibus ingenium, & ungues ad hoc natura tribuit. Aliae cavernas, & specus impetrosis quaeritant, & ubi non inveniunt, nemorum, fruticumque congerie aedificant impenetrabiles etiam imbribus, si Plinio credas. Arborum aliae cava subeunt. Et denique fera omnia latibulorum opacitate delectantur, atque recreantur imprimis. Et veluti lucem oderint dies totos latitant, noctibus vero prodeunt. Sed neque domestici greges pecoris, nec armenta stabulorum lucem desyderant, salubriusque pascuntur in obscuro. Quinetiam volucres quibus natura caelum assignavit, lucos tamen praecipue, & frondosa nemorum, umbrosaque convallium incolunt, nisi cum ad requirendos cibos evolitant. Omne porro genus aquilarum, & accipitrum, quod vel maxime ferum est, nulla re magis, quam tenebris cicuratur. His enim aucupes statim a captura palpebras oculorum insuunt ad aliquot dies. Et avibus ita mansuefactis, his praecipue quas dicunt altivolas capita concludunt scorteis cucullis, ne lucem videant eminente solum rostro. Et ita conditis oculis, haerentes pugno, feritate naturali deposita, circunferuntur quietissime. Est etiam natura comparatum ut animalia caetera praeter hominem aliquatenus in tenebris, & caligine cernant. Quare magna rerum imperitia, nec fine temeritate lapsi videntur, qui citra necessitatem, & contra Domini praescriptum fenestras in arca plures astruunt. Unam autem solum in praecepto positam dicere, quae omnium maxima foret, perinde vanum est ac si dicas, plures arculas divino iussu fabricatas, sed unius arce tantum fieri mentionem, quae grandior esset. De fenestrae mensura nihil scriptum est, nisi quis forte putet (sicut recentiores quidam tempore nostro in suis adnotationibus hebraicis posuerunt) id quod sequitur: Et in cubito consummabis altitudinem eius, ad ipsius fenestram modum pertinere, propter amphibolon relationis in pronomine eius, ad arcam, vel fenestram in propinquo positas. Quod item ambiguum graecus fermo recipit in αὐτὴν pronomine ad fenestram relato. Quanquam locus in exemplaribus graecis corrupte legitur habens ἐπισυνάγων participium, ubi θυείδα, hoc est fenestram debuit. Esset enim sensus ad literam, congregans, sive coniungens facies in arca. Quem prosus ineptum esse quis non videt: Sic etiam fenestra tolleretur ab o-/10/pere. Sed amphiboliam statim soluit hebraica dictio Thecalena, ubi syllaba finalis, na, est pronomen generis foeminini, significans eam, affixum verbo Thecale, quod est consummabis, quod quidem na, nequaquam referri potest ad Soer, id est fenestram, cum semper dicatur Soer apud Hebraeos genere masculino. Et si ad Soer, fieret relatio: dicendum erat Thecalenu. Ipsum praeterea verbum consummabis, sive perficies, aliquid iam inchoatum, nec adhuc completum innuit. Quodquidem est arca, tantisper imperfecta dum habeat operculum, id est tectum. cuius nullibi praeterquam in his verbis praeceptum invenies. Arcam igitur in cubito perfici, intelligo praeter caeteros omnes, ut cubitus iste sit altitudo mediana culminis per totam longitudine cubitorum tercentum, praeter ecphoras. Quaequidem altitudo longioris etiam tractus profluvio satis erat, in planitie praesertim levigata, asphaltoque lubrica. Etenim Vitruvius ipse in eo solo rivi, quo per canales structiles aqua ducitur, libramenta fieri statuit fastiga ta ducentesima tantum parte longitudinis. In hac autem positione tecti fastigium cubitale ratione Vitruvii octuplo superat. Praeter id etiam quae caelestis aqua deciduis undique guttis seipsa propellens facilius multo labitur, quam quae rivo, vel canali procedit. Ad hunc igitur quem dixi modum constituta summitas unius altitudine cubiti, nulla relinquitur in culmine latitudo, quam omnes quos huc usque legerim ista disputantes cubitalem esse voluerunt. Unde quatuor formis invicem differentibus figuratio processit inopere, quarum pseudographias cum figuratione quam institui simul ostendam in sequentibus, ubi quod est reliquum in descriptione perpendero. Hic autem orthographiam geminae frontis secundum latum & altum arcae disposui, ubi linea B A fastigium cubitale designat.

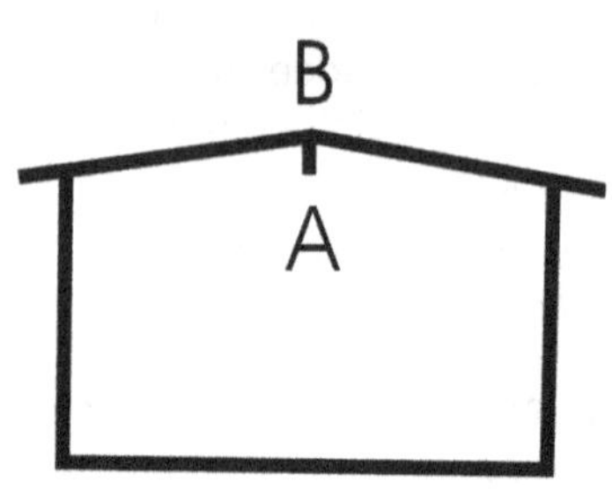

VII. De Ostio, & Coenaculis.

QUOD autem habet lectio vulgata, Ostium arcae pones ex latere, deorsum, coenacula, & tristega facies in ea. Si deorsum ad antecedentia referatur: contra veritatem Hebraicam erit. Si autem ad sequentia, id est ad coenacula: repugnabit significatio vocis. Quandoquidem coenaculum (teste Varrone) locus est ubi coenabatur. Sed postquam in superiori parte coenitari coeptum est: superior domus uniuersa coenacula dicta. Quod etiam confirmat Vitruvius, ita scribens. Cum /11/ enim aucto mirum immodum populo Romano necesse fuisset in coenaculis habitari, ad aedificiorum, altitudines deventum est. Et Cicero de lege agraria dicit,

Romam in montibus positam, & coenaculis sublatam, atque suspensam. Hic igitur coenacula vertisse non minus est incongruens, quam superiora si dicas pro inferiora. Et verbum tristega grecum est, idem quod tria tuguria, quo tamen interpretes septuaginta non ututur, sed ita dicunt. κατάγαια διώφορα καὶ τριώφορα hoc est, apothecas duorum tabulatorum & trium tabulatorum. Est autem apotheca proprie inferior, atque grandior cella ubi fructus, & fruges servandi gratia conduntur. In qua significatione Plinius saepe, & Columella sunt usi. Et proposito nostro mire conveniunt huiusmodi conditoria ad animalium victum. Sed ne totas apothecas in locis inferioribus esse secundum significati proprietatem crederet aliquis, adiicitur, duorum tabulatorum, & trium tabulatorum. Nam sicut domino iubente omnis generis commeatus in arcam sunt importati: sic aliis, atque aliis tabulatis seorsum, distincteque recondi necessarium erat: non ad conservationem tantum, scilicet ne permistione confusa putrescerent: sed etiam ad dispensandi commoditatem. Quod autem interpretes quidam novi vertunt inferiora, & secunda, & tertia facies. Quid rogo confuse magis, nulloque sensu dici potuit? quam sic per adiectiva loqui sine substantivis. Caeterum super ostii positione quod dicitur, ex obliquo, hanc intelligere debes a dextra, vel a sinistra parte longitudinis arcae, prope latera, qui sunt anguli, non autem, plana: vel (ut ita dicam) parietes, quibus arca compingitur, sicut intellexerunt praepostere multi. Hoc etiam eleganter diceretur a latere, vel ad latus, non autem ex latere, vel in latere, prout aliqui dixerunt. Quis enim vidit unquam ostium in ipso angulo poni. Haec fere nobis de scripti formula constant. Quae cum sit angusta verbis, sensu diffusa, ex paucis alia multa rationibus architectonicis, coniecturaque solerti, sunt investiganda: ut operis tam praeclari cognitionem omni diligentia plenius assequamur.

VIII. De Cubitis & Eorum Mensura.

CUBITORUM numerus per quos arcae moduli finiuntur traditione certus est: sed ipsorum longitudo opinionibus incerta. Dicunt enim multi (sicut verum est) cubitum sesquipede finiri. Ad hoc alii semipedem adiiciunt, auctoritate tamen nulla probantes. Alii porro multi ad pedes usque novem extenderunt. Aliis postremo & pedem, & cubitum, non ut nunc, sed ut olim cum grandiora fuerunt corpora modis quidem grandioribus, sed incertis aestimare visum est. Cum autem in literis sacris cubitorum sit mentio frequens: non plus tamen quam semel eorum mensuram invenio designari. Quanquam vix etiam satis aperte. Locus est Deuteronomii capite tertio, de Og rege Basan, qui solus restiterat de stirpe gigantum: ubi scribitur lectus eius ferreus novem cubitos habuisse longitudinis, & quatuor latitudinis, ad mensuram cubiti virilis. Hoc ultimum sic exponit interpretatio graeca ejn phvcei ajndrovV, hoc est in cubito viri. Extenditur autem cubitus ab articulo medio brachii ad extremum medium digitum usque, nunquam excedens /12/ pedem & dimidium in viro qui bene sit a natura figuratus, nec asymmetros. Id etiam Vitruvius in terminandis mensuris probatissimus author, exemplis graecorum multis confirmat, cubitum scilicet constare sex palmis. Palmos autem quatuor efficere pedem, & digitos quatuor contineri palmo. Et hominem ita commodulari, ut sit cubitus pars staturae quarta, pes vero sexta. Certum est aute latinos dimensiones a graecis sicut alia bona multa sumpsisse, Graeci autem ab Aegyptiis usurparunt, authores tamen ubique dissimulando. In his autem Hebraei Aegyptios instituisse feruntur. Ipse autem Moses dimetiens arcam, & Hebraeorum, & Aegyptiorum sapientiam omnem optime calluit. Omnes etiam Hebraeorum Rabini super huiusmodi cubitis sesquipedalibus inter se conveniunt. Sane de cubitis, pedibus, palmis, digitis, & aliis id genus ab humano corpore mensuris quod post diluvium una cum suo toto decreverint, probabiliter fortasse dixeris. Sed quatenus incertum. Nostri porro scriptores orthodoxi videntes ordinationem opificis summi haereticorum calumniis agitari, & in angustum deduci, contradicendo putarunt modulum istum cubitalem sexcuplo, quam dixi maiorem, id est novem pedum fuisse. Et haec obtinuit in universum opinio, nemine quem viderim contradicente, quamvis tali mensurae non pauca de scripturis loca repugnent, quorum nunc unum, & alterum subiiciam. Legitur in libris regum de Goliath Philisthaeo quod statura fuerit alta sex cubitis, & palmo. Quos si contendas novem pedum fuisse: erat altitudo Goliath pedum quinquaginta quatuor, & palmi. Quare & caput ipsius, secundum corporis humani symmetrias, pedum fere novem, ad quam proceritatem communis hominum corporatura non pertingit. Quomodo igitur David caput hostis abscisum seipso grandius in manu sua (sicut scriptum est) coram Saule tenuisset? Ad haec etiam in Exodo, cum iubetur altare fieri trium cubitorum altitudine, non possunt intelligi grandiores isti, pedum scilicet vigintiseptem fuisse. Sic enim nullus erat sacrificiis usus, nisi scalis admotis ad aram. Quod a ritu sacrorum abhorret omnino. De hac autem extensione cubitorum unde processerit, & quantus sit error, postea dicam. ubi fidem veris, & usitatis sesquipedalibus cubitis per ea quae prius super operis fabricatione particulatim sunt exquirenda firmavero. Nam & hanc quoque rationem haereticorum alia factio (cuius etiam divus meminit Augustinus libro decimo quinto de civitate Dei) naturali, diversaque malignitate ludificavit, ineptissime disputando tantae magnitudinis arcam non posse compingi. Cuius ego contrarium architectonica methodo breviter ostendam. Quam partem aliquantulum obscuram his scio fore, qui sensus in istiusmodi literis non habent exercitatos.

IX. De Arcae Structura, Quomodo Fieri Potuit.

ATQUE ut a fundamentis exordium sumam, sitque commensuum explicatio commodior, dicamus arcae basim ad rationem cubiti sesquipedalis longuam fuisse pedes quadringentos quinquaginta, latam vero pedes septuaginta quinque, altitudinem vero totam in arca, praeter cubitale fastigium habuisse pedes quadraginta quinque. Scien-/13/dum est autem has mensuras omnes citra materiae crassitudinem intra opus ipsum accipi debere. Et cum in fabricatione tota firmitatis ratio sit habenda diligenter, tum in basi potissimum, in quam oneris pondus universi, & moles aedificii tota recumbit. Hanc igitur cum reliqua superstructione simul iis rationibus factam, vel certe fieri posse nullus scio nisi rerum prorsus, & artis ignarus negare poterit. Primum enim centum trabes perpetuae sesquipedales quadratae secundum totam strati latitudinem aequalibus inter se spaciis collocabantur. Duas tamen extrema latera basis minora facientes aliquanto caeteris esse crassiores oportuit. Has insuper palmopedalia tigna in transversum ordine duplici, ad utraque trabium capita incisuris ad mediam crassitudinem sesquipedalibus factis, firmiter distinebant, relictis tamen dextra, sinistraque trabium proiecturis: in quas arrectariorum pedalium, angulariorum vero bipedalium bases securiclatis cardinibus immitterentur. Omnium autem capita superne cardinatis trabibus concludebantur. Ipsae autem trabes in summo quatuor laterariis duodecim pedum longitudine sub angulos oblique fixis, anconibusque ferreis vinctae continebantur. Solum deinde basis supra trabes bessali materia contexebatur. Arrectaria quoque per circuitum forinsecus postes transuersi trientales vestiebnat. Intra vero catenationibus, praecinctionibusque valide continebantur. Insuper his compactilia transtra septem aequalibus spaciis inter se, duoque latera minora in latitudinem procurrendo supremis trabibus adglutinata oram arcae superiorem validissime firmabant. Ac nihilosecius quatuordecim columnae ligneae altitudinibus a fundo perpetuis ascendentes transtra binae singula fulciebant. Quibus duae singulis hinc inde parastatae cohaerentes, una cum aliis pedamentorum fulturis contignationem primam in quatuor cubitorum altitudinem sustolebant. Hanc autem duae sequebantur, mediana quidem altitudine cubitorum octo, suprema deinde intervallo cubitorum decem a media. Quas & parastatae circa columnas, aliaeque fulturae inferiorum perpendiculo respondentes sustinebant. Super media transtra, duoque latera minora novem scapi altitudine cubitales columen fastigii, una cum capreolis excipiebant. Unde canterii dextra, sinistraque proclinati extra longiora superioris orae latera prominebant aequaliter. Quibus coassatio superimposita aedificium tegebat, ipsaeque subgrundae stillicidium extra perpendiculum arcae propellebant.

X. De Contignationum Usibus.

USUS contabulationum talis erat: ut super prima quadrupedum omnium, atque reptilium cubilia, sive nidi vocentur, suo cuiusque generi commoda locarentur, assamentis, cancellisque conclusa: & ambulationibus in longum, transversumque dispositis, per quas possent homines facile cuncta prospicere, & usui necessaria suppeditare. Quinetiam opus fuit in stratis ipsis aperturas, & foramina relinqui, per quae prolaberentur in arcae fundum, velut in sentinam excrementa. Qui /14/ totus necessitatibus his cubitorum quatuor altitudine vacabat. Nisi forte aliquid ibidem saburrae (sicut exigit ratio navigandi) positum esset. Inter mediam, supremamque contignationem omnis generis anno, nam pro subiectis animalibus apothecae continebant, duobus, aut tribus singulae tabulatis intra se distinctae. Cuius rei causam supra retulimus. Nec eadem oportuit omnes magnitudine factas, sed pro ratione commeatuum quos asservabant temperari. Utpote foenilia, palearia, & quae frondes asseruabant capaciora, quam granaria, & etiam his quae glandem, nuces, iuglandem, castaneas habebant. Et rursus in quibus pabulum fuit, differentiam tabulata separabant: veluti foeni verni, & autumnalis, quod dicitur cordum, farraginis, viciae, medicae, foeni graeci, erui, cicerculae. Et in aliis itidem ubi fruges condebantur granorum, leguminumque species secernebantur tabulatis. Semitas praeterea apothecis interponi commodissimum fuit. Et in ipsis foramina superstantia directe praesepiis. ut inde victus animalibus, etiam in aliquot dies facile ministraretur. Quibus etiam potus aliquot epistomiis, vel siphonibus (quos vocant mechanici diabetes) canaliculisque in stabula singulorum derivantibus aquam, paulo momento dispensabatur. In media regione suprema amplum coenaculum fuit, hominum habitatio, illuminatum arcae fenestra. quae cum grandior esset: valuas habuit, speculari lapide, seu vitro, crystallove munitas, ut iniuriam caeli, non diem arcerent. Coenaculo iungebatur cella penaria, atque culina, cui focus erat lapideo tabulatu, molaeque trusatiles, cum clibanis ibi etiam erant. Item andronitis, atque ginaeceum, duo scilicet cubicula, unum virorum, & alterum mulierum seorsum fuere distincta. Communis nempe doctorum sententia tenet, maritos ab uxoribus seorsum in arca semper cubuisse. Haec autem membra secundarium lumen (ut vocant Optici) a coenaculo capiebant. In aliis vero quoties opus erat, lucernarum usus adhibebatur. Prope culinam lignile fuit, ex lignis coctis, quae dicuntur acapna, id est sine fumo. Et insuper carbonaria cella. Familiares autem cellae in haram porcorum tubulo ferebantur. Post haec horreum sequebatur, & apothecae fructibus rusticis omne genus refertae. Atque deinceps aliae cibis avium dicatae. Quarum omnium ornithones, & caveae in hac contabulatione suprema fuerunt, viarumque directiones, intermissis iuncturarum modice spaciis, ut essent velut aestuaria, quibus refrigesceret aër, subiectorum animalium halitu calefactus, essetque spiramentum salubrius. Ad hoc etiam habuit ora superior ab utraque longitudinis parte spiracula, operis quadam necessitate relicta, prohibente scilicet canteriorum crassitudine, ne trabibus arrectariorum transversis asseres supremi iungerentur. Unde tamen propter subgrundiorum ecphoras, nec lumen, nec omnino pluvialis aqua descendebat in arcam. Scalas insuper locis opportunis adhibitas nihil est dubitandum, per quas aditus facilis ad omnia tabulata pateret. Vectorum praeterea, & onerum distributionem ita factam intelligas, ut navigium super aquis per librata positione ferretur. Cuius figura longior, sicut oneri ferundo commoda fuit, ita & huiusmodi temperamento opus habebat praecipue. /15/

XI. De Trabium Materie.

SI quis forte contenderit latitudinem, vel altitudinem aedificii una continuitate, tenoreque trabium iungi non posse, sicut antea posui: quod ad id magnitudinis materia non crescit. Historiam mundi legat, & inveniet Hyrcaniae sylvae arborum vastitate miracula supra fidem. Et in quibusdam insulis arborum proceritatem ad centum quadraginta quatuor pedes adolescere. Amplissimam arborum Plinius ad aevum suum Romae visam existimat, quam propter miraculum Tyberius Caesar ponte naumachiario exposuerat. Fuit autem trabs e larice longa pedes centum viginti, bipedali crassitudine aequalis. Quo intelligebatur (inquit) vix credibilis reliqua altitudo, fastigium ad cacumen aestimantibus. Alia in Cypro traditur ad undeciremem Demetrii succisa, centum triginta pedum longitudinis, crassitudinis vero, ad trium hominum complexum. Sed quid attinet veterum testimonio fidem e longinquo petere? cum ipsi plerumque videamus in Delphinaticis nostratium montibus abietes octoginta pedibus altiores.

XII. De Ostii Positura, & Nidis.

OSTIUM autem arcae in infimo poni propter sentinam non erat commodum. Sed ita ut ad contignationem primam ubi fuerunt animalia limen haberet, & in ipso limine cardines, unde fores versatae proclinarentur in terram, scalarumque vicem supplerent quatuor cubitorum ascensu. Vult tamen Hugo, qui super arca Noe tractatum aedidit, ostium non prope fundum, sicut dixi, sed altius fuisse collocatum, in ea parte navigii quae staret ab aquis. Ita ut foris (inquit) per aquas ad arcam accedentibus ostium fere per planum occurreret. Cuius sententiam ego probarem, si constaret animalia invalescente iam diluvio ad arcam enatasse. Sed ante diluvii principia (sicut scriptum est) ipsi homines, & omne animal secundum genus suum ingressa sunt ad Noe in arcam, occlusitque dominus ostium foris. Prope est etiam ut de claudentis diligentia dubitent, qui ianuae commissuras aquis committere non audeant. Idem etiam author, & alii tradunt nidos, sive mansiunculas non intra arcam, sed extra fuisse, ad excipiendum id animalium genus, quae Graeci vocant amphibia, propter id quod non tantum terrestria, sed aquatilia quoque defyderant pabula, nec magis humo, quam stagno consueverunt, quorum est ancer, mergus, & anas, cignus, alcyones, & aliae quaedam aviculae: quadrupedum vero cocodrilus, lutra, fiber, & alia pauca, existimantes tale genus inclusum servari non potuisse. Quod certe falsum est. Huiusmodi enim vitam facile tollerant extra aquas, etiam quae piscibus vescuntur, dum carnes habeant loco piscium. Vidi enim aliquando dum essem Lutetiae duos pisces, ex his qui dicuntur vituli marini curru vectos elonginquo ad regem nostrum, spectaculi gratia, qui non minus avide carnes, /16/ quam pisces vorabant. Potuit etiam si piscibus erat opus in cibum, fieri intra arcam piscina, sicut in illa Syculorum regis Hieronis nave memorabili factum legimus. In qua fuit aedificii contignatio triplex, apparatus materiae triremium sexaginta, remigationis vero ordinum viginti. Et quod ad propositum spectat, sic Atheneus scribit. Erat (inquit) ad proram receptaculum aquae conclusum, capiens duo milia metretas assamentis, pice, lintheisque compositum. Prope hoc etiam erat piscina, laminis plumbeis, assibusque compacta, aquae marinae plena, ubi commode multi pisces alebantur. Caeterum qui extra arcam amphibiis loculamenta disponunt, viderint ipsi quomodo se contra domini praescriptum tueantur, ita iubentis: Ex cunctis animantibus universae carnis bina induces in arcam, ut vivant tecum. & rursum: Bina de omnibus ingredientur tecum, ut possint vivere. Quod & postea factum scriptura repetit, dicens: Ex omni quod movetur super terram duo, & duo ingressa sunt ad Noe in arcam.

XIII. De Carnivoris Animantibus.

NULLUM animal ex carnivoris in arca cibatu suo victitasse theologi omnes uno ore consentiunt. Quoniam (ut dicunt) sine mandati transgressione fieri non potuit, ut praeter numerum datum a Domino in arca fuissent animalia, quae aliorum alendorum necessitas coegisset includi. Et magis esse credendum, ibi praeter carnes alimenta fuisse, quae omnibus convenirent. Nam (ut divus ait Augustinus) animalia multa quibus caro cibus est, fructibus, pomisque vescuntur, maxime fico, & castaneis: & omnibus vesci cogit fames, & nihil esse quod Deus suave, & salubre facere non possit, qui etiam ut sine cibo viverent praestare potuit. Ad haec dico breviter, animalia quorum datus est numerus, ea fuisse quae sponte ingressa sunt in arcam. ut quemadmodum scriptum est, cum ipso Noe vivere possent, & eorum semen servaretur super faciem universae terrae. Alia vero cibi gratia comparata sub universali mandato contineri, ubi dictum est: Tolles igitur tecum ex omnibus escis quae mandi possunt, & comportabis apud te, & erunt tam tibi quam illis in cibum.

Quomodo igitur universalis iussionis summam Noe complevisset, carnes praetermittendo: quibus solis ferarum, volucrumque bona pars vescitur. Aut quis unquam admittat, leonoes, lupos, pardos, tigrides, necnon aquilarum, accipitrumque genera, & omnes denique volucres, quae rostro sunt, & pedibus uncis, fructibus, & pomis, atque castaneis annum totum potuisse vivere? Porro de alimentis quae omnibus conveniunt, res planae ficta est. Nec de potestate divina quicquam ambigimus. Sed nunc quid Deus ipse iussit, non quid possit quaeritur. Ipse igitur dispensator carnibus comportatis ad Domini mandatum nihil adiectione peccavit, quin potius his omissis multum detractione peccabat. /17/

XIV. De Fabris, & Operariis Arcae.

QUAERUNT nonnulli quomodo tantae molis, & tam operosum navigium a quatuor hominibus, scilicet Noe, & tribus filiis perfici potuit, centum etiam annorum spatio, quibus fabricationem durasse scriptura testatur. Ad quod dicamus cum Augustino, adhibitos insuper alios operi fabros. Et revera in aedificationibus magnis non solum operarum, sed etiam operariorum multitudo requiritur. Propterea quod incidunt multa quae pauci tractare non satis commode possunt. Esset autem absurdum dubitare, ut is quem praefectum operi suo Deus elegit, ne non simul cum arte, atque prudentia, facultates etiam acceperit: sine quibus nihil promovebatur operis effectus. Non tamen negaverim quin Noe architecti funges officio, cum tribus filiis fabris, & aliquot administris tempore centum annorum opus absolvere potuerit. Quod perinde vale acsi tercentum fabros cum ministerio subserviente, uno anno tenuisset in opere. Constat enim authore Plutarcho Hieronem regem, navigium illud quod paulo supra memoravi, cum iam advecta esset materia ex Aetna monte, intra duodecim menses consummavisse, adhibitis operi faciundo tercentum fabris, praeter administros fabricae subservientes, praefecto summae operis architecto Archia Corinthio. Perspectis igitur quae ad aedificii qualitatem pertinebant, superest ut ea prosequamur, quae ad quantitatem intelligendam praecipue faciunt.

XV. De Arcae Capacitate.

UT AUTEM in his quae deinceps calculo geometrico sum traditurus, constitutis, certisque modis omnia constent, semipedis longitudinem hic apposui, ducta linea recta B A, cuius lineae duplum eum pedem constituit, quem Parrisienses regium vocant, eoque in privatis, & publicis operibus utuntur. Quare & eiusdem lineae B A triplum, faciet cubitum sesquipedalem, quem ego symmetriarum in arca nostra modulum constituo, ad certam ipsius quantitatem habendam. Esto linea recta b c, quam ponamus esse cubitum, qualem iam constitui, & ex ipsa b c describatur quadratum D. Item ex eadem linea describatur cubus M. Quadratum igitur D, erit cubitus quadratus. Cubus vero M erit cubitus solidus, siue corporeus, quem etiam cubitale cubum vocamus. Ut autem habeas cubicationem in arca, hoc est totam quantitatem corpoream, quae est capacitas ipsius. Quaere primum embadon basis, quae & quadratura dicitur, multiplicando longitudinis cubitos tercentum, in latitu-/18/dinis cubitos quinquaginta, fiunt cubiti quadrati quindecim millia. Hanc summam rursum multiplica in altitudinis cubitos triginta, fiunt cubita solida quatercentum quinquaginta millia, quod est solidum interius arcae, usque ad suggrundas. Residuum autem corporis ad tectum, cum sit prisma, continet dimidium sui parallelepipedi, id est cubita septem millia quingenta. Adde ad quatercentum quinquaginta millia, sit summa totius arcae in cubitalibus cubis, quatercentum quinquaginta septem millia quingenta. Sed quoniam huiusmodi capacitas aliquibus impedimentis occupatur, veluti sunt columnae cum suis parastatis, tabulatorum etiam crassitudo, & assamenta distinguentia nidos & apothecas. Ista compensabimus prismatis corpore, a dicta quantitate deducto. Restat igitur capacitas in arca quatercentum quinquaginta millium cubitorum. Quam magnitudinem ad animalium omnium semina servanda largiter sufficere monstrabo.

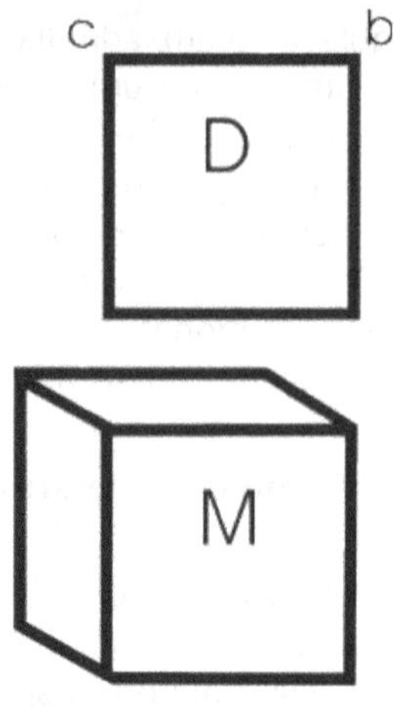

XVI. Animalium Recensio Nominatim Per Genera.

CUM iam aedificii formam, dispositionis ordinem, atque magnitudinem, architectonicis, geometricisque methodis tractaverimus: non parva superest in propositio difficultas ostendere, quemadmodum arcae magnitudo iam data omnium quae sunt in terris animantium genera, cum annuis singulorum alimentis intra se recipiat. Istud enim praecipue cavillantur haeretici. Ad haec igitur investigatione facta sedulo, secundum historias omnium quibus curae fuit posteris ista mandare, quadrupedum genera nominatim infra dispona, septenarii, binariique numero munda discernens ab immundis. Explosa est enim communiter illorum sententia qui numeros istos in hac differentia duplicarunt. Et quoniam non omnes omnibus species oculis, aut literis sunt exploratae: ipsas in tria maxime genera nota, comparatione distribuam: quae sunt boves, & oves, atque lupi. Quae sane digestio ad intelligentiam rei praecipue valet. Terrestrium autem omnium (author Plinio) maximum est elephas. Et secundum Aristotelem bove maior quadruplo. Propterea elephantes duos ratione magnitudinis, atque victus, ad locum occupandum, pono valere boves octo. In Hercynia sylva sunt ferae, qui Uri appellantur, magnitudine paulo infra elephantes, specie & colore Thauri: de quibus neque Plinius, nec animalium historia meminit, sed Caesar in commentariis. Nec sunt inter animalia munda numerandi. Quoniam ex feris (inquit Aristoteles) nullum adhuc ruminare constat dempto cervo. Aequiparabimus itaque Uros duos bobus sex. In eadem sylva bos est cervi figura unicornis, de quo etiam Caesar in commentariis. Pro his igitur pono boves duos. Quatuor sunt /19/ genera camelorum, Arabica scilicet, & Bactriana, & quae dicitur Dromeda. Item cameleopardalis. Hae simul fiunt paria quatuor, valore autem boves sedecim. Rhinocerotes duo, aestimatione vero boves quatuor. Monocerotes, duo. Bisontes, duo. Bubali, duo. Bonasi, duo. Origes, ii. Tarandi, ii. Equi pennati, & cornigeri quos dicunt pegasos, ii. Boves Indici unicornes, & solidis ungulis, ii. Struthiocameli, ii. bestiarum potius quam avium generis, ad hoc demum datis pennis ut currentes adiuvent, caetero non sunt volucres. Domestici boves, septem. Cervi, septem, aequiparatione vero boves quatuor. Tragelaphi, hoc est hircocervi, septem, valore boves quatuor. Hipelaphi, ii. Equi domestici, ii. Equi feri, ii. Hippardia, ii. Hippopotami, hoc est, fluviatiles equi, ii. Asini, ii. Onagri, ii. Asini Indici unicornes, ii. Ursi, ii. Sues, ii. Apri, ii. Huiusmodi autem animalia cuncta pabulo, frugibusque vescuntur, aut simul ambobus, aut separatim altero. In quibus autem non apponitur aestimatio, pro pari boum sumenda sunt. Quamquam sit in aliquibus adiectione, in nullis autem detractione peccatum. Haec igitur omnia proportione respondent boum paribus quadragintaquinque & dimidio. Caeterum si quid nunc vel diligentiam nostram, vel eorum, qui precedentibus saeculis ista pervestigarunt forte fefellerit: per causam quasi supplementi ex invento numero 45 1/2 sexaginta boum paria faciemus.

XVII. Animalium Nomina Minorum, Quae Pabulo Etiam Frugibusque Vescuntur.

ARIETUM & ovium, tam ex mansuetis, quam feris quatuor esse genera leguntur. Quae si omnia munda sunt, explent numerum septenarium quater, hoc est fiunt oves viginti octo. Caprae etiam in plurimas similitudines transfigurantur: veluti sunt caprae domesticae, & ex feris dictae capreae, atque rupicaprae. Sunt item Ibices, pernicitatis mirandae, onerato capite vastis cornibus. Sunt & Origes, contrario pilo vestiti ad caput verso. Praeterea Damae, & Pigargi, & Strepsi corotes. Haec autem octo genera vix est ut sint omnia munda: quoniam (ut anteadixi) nullum ex feris animal constat ruminare dempto ceruo. Propterea caprinum genus universum aestimo ad oves triginta. Simiarum praeterea genus aliquot differentiis variatur, ut est Simia, Caebus, Cynocephalus, Cercopitecus, & id genus alia, pro quibus oves pono decem. Lepus, ii. Lepus candidus in alpibus degens, ii. Dasypus ex leporum genere, ii. Cuniculus domesticus, ii. Cuniculus ferus, ii. Melis alias Taxo, ii. Sciurus, ii. Glis, ii. Est etiam murium genus multiplex, inter quos talpas enumero. Quamquam sunt qui putent mures in arca non suisse, & id genus similia, propterea quod ex corruptione nascantur, sicut nec etiam mulos: quoniam ex alio genere procreantur. Herinacei, ii. Histrices, ii. Haec igitur animalia minura, a lepore posterius enumerata, ponimus valere oves quatuor. Quare ex supradictis omnibus summa crescit ad ovium paria quadraginta. /20/

XVIII. Animalium Nomina Quae Carnibus Vescuntur.

INTER carnivoras animantes notissimus est lupus, ad hunc igitur de caeteris comparatio fiet. Leones duo. Pardi, ii. Leucocrutae a sini fere magnitudine, ii. Calae, ii. Dracones, ii. Serpentes boe, ii. Ista sex paria singula aestimo lupis quatuor. Fiunt igitur lupi quatuor & viginti. Tauri cornua habentes mobilia venatu viventes, ii. Manticorae humani corporis vel precipue appetentes, ii. Pro duobus his paribus pono lupos duodecim. Pantherae, ii. Tigrides, ii. Lupi, ii. Lupi canarii, ii. Lupi cervarii, qui & thoes dicuntur,ii. Chai, ii. Cephae, ii. Linces, ii. Sphinges, ii. Crocutae, ii. Axes ferae, ii. Parva quaedam animalia victum ab aquis petunt, sic tamen ut in terra degant, quorum nomina sunt haec, Latax, Fiber, Satherium, Satyrum, Lutra: huiusmodi quinque paria aequiparo lupis duobus. Hiena, quam alii glavum vocant. Lycaon, Vulpes, Feles, Ichneumon, Viverra, vulgo furetus. Mustella. In istorum septem paribus cum sint corpore modica, aestimationem facio, ad duos lupos. Vituli marini pennis quibus in mari utuntur, humi quoque vice pedum serpunt, ii. Omnium igitur supradictorum summa facit luporum paria triginta duo. Sed in supplementum pone, ut sint paria quadraginta.

XIX. Dispensatio Victus Pro Carnivoris, Stabulationisque Omnium Dispositio, Cum Ichnographia.

CARNIVORAS animantes ad luporum paria quadraginta recensui, singulis autem paribus ad victum quatridui ovem unam constituo. Absumuntur ergo pro cibariis omnium oves quotidie decem. Quas multiplicando in anni dies tercentum sexaginta quinque fiunt annuo cibatu oves tria millia sexcentum quinquaginta. His ita constitutis, superest ut ostendam quemadmodum omnes superius enumeratae quadrupedes, hoc est boves centum viginti, Oves tria millia septingentae triginta. Lupi octoginta, stabulavi possint in ea contignatione (sicut antea dixi) quae cubitis quatuor distat a basi, a mediana autem cubitis octo. Primum iam ab ostio, quod viginti cubitis ad angulum arcae dispono, via lata sex cubitos in totam lateris longitudinem procurrebat, scalis utrinque in superiora ferentibus terminata. Ad cuius medium, alia tertia parte latior rectis angulis consistens opposito lateri iungebatur, nidos sexaginta rectangulos longitudine cubitorum quinque latitudine vero trium cum duabus tertiis disterminans aequaliter in duas partes, utrinque productos ad viam primam inter se contigue, nisi quod diverticulis duobus medianum iter recte secantibus distinguebantur, in sex veluti consepta, loculamentisque suis decussata. Quibus singula singulis boum paria collocari possent. Inter quae tamen necesse fuit aliqua fieri laxiora proportione beluarum magnitudinis, ut pote duo-/21/rum elephantorum stabulum, sicut boum paribus quatuor aestimantur: ita & nidos quatuor occupare debuit. Alia deinde quadraginta minorum animalium paria diversi generis, ovili magnitudine censita, nidis suis rectangulis longitudine tricubitali, serie etiam bipartita latitudinem tabulati ad viam usque iungebant, interstitio viarum duplici, aequalique, & aequidistante mediano, a maioribus separata. Ad haec rursum alia totidem parium pro carnivoris stabulatio dextra, sinistraque ovilibus cohaerabat, pari nidorum latitudine, sed excedente longitudine cubito. Quorum ordines terminabant duo limites cubitorum quatuor amplitudine, satis commodi per quos ministrarentur ipsis carnivoris oves in cibum. Idque ab ipsarum ovium caulis duabus utrinque quod reliquum fuit contignationis occupantibus, ambarum longitudine simul ducentum viginti octo cubitorum, latitudine autem communi cubitorum quatuor & quadraginta. Quaequidem dimensio, claudit decem millia triginta duo cubitalium quadratorum. Quae si distribuantur ad oves

cibarias tria millia sexcentas quinquaginta: provenit in parte singulis paribus quadratura pauxillo minor quinque cubitis cum semisse. Est autem non ab re sciendum oves istas in cibum aliter vel in arcae summo, vel in imo, & etiam alibi, si cogeret aliqua necessitas posse stabulari. Et ita duplo quam recensui maiorem nidorum, animaliumque numerum contignatio prima reciperet: cuius ichnographiam hic apposui.

XX. De Ratione Victus Animantium Caeterarum Quae Non Sunt Carnivorae.

SATIS iam demonstrasse videor omnis generis quadrupedes, tam ad vitam sibi, quam ad victum alienum in una contignationem arcae, magno etiam laxamento posse constitui. Quod ad disputationem susceptam nondum satis erit, nisi & apothecarum cibaria in amni vertentis usum sufficere probavero. Animal fere nullum est pabulo vescens, cui non sit etiam frugum appetentia maior. Quarum commeatus angustius, & expeditius multo quam ipsius pa-/22/buli conduntur. Quod dico tale est: Decem pondo foeni, aut viciae pabularis multo plus loci tenebunt, quam decem pondo hordei, aut viciae seminalis. Et quae mensura foeni ad vitam tolleranda bovi satis erit in diem, eadem mensura farris, siue farraginis, cuiuslibetve grani, biduo, vel triduo ad saginam etiam corporis exuberabit. Sed quo validius arcae capacitate ab adversariorum calumniis asseramus, demonstrabitur tantum in ea foeni potuisse recondi, qui cibus est omnium impeditissimus, quantum ad vitam animalium tuendam large suppetit in annum. Iam enim in praecedentibus animalium grandiorum corpora magnitudine peraequata redegimus ad paria boum sexaginta, qui fiunt boves centum viginti. Minorum autem quae servantur in semen, ad oves octoginta. Aliarum autem multitudo quas pro cibatu carnario posui, sicut decade subducta quotidie decrescit: ita & ipsarum cibatus ab anni summa decrescere debent. Quo fit, ut iam dictus numerus gregis tria millia sex centum quinquaginta, non plus impendat in annum, quam numero semper eodem oves mille octingentae viginti. Huius porro supputationis formulam, cum non sit exposita vulgo, alias explicui in opere logistico. Ad has igitur cibarias oves mille octingentas viginti, adde alias octoginta, fit ovium utraque summa mille noningentae. Sane quo fiat expeditior calculus seques, pone septem oves, quod ad ventris, alimentorumque rationem spectat aestimari bove. Igitur oves mille nongentae, valent bobus trecentis nonaginta uno, cum tribus septimis unius. Iunge ad boves centum viginti, fit summa boum trecentum nonaginta unius, cum tribus septimis. Sed ut abunde sint omnia, pono boves esse quadringentos in arca, qui foeno pratensi tantum, inundationis tempore toto saturari debeant. Porro cum foeni demensum quotidianum singulis bobus inquirerem, experimento didici verissimum esse quod tradit Columella, rerum rusticarum scientissimus author. Ianuario scilicet mensae satis esse singulis bobus foeni pondo triginta. Martio, & Aprili quia terra proscinditur, sat esse pondo quadraginta singulis dari. Certum est pondo idem esse quae libram unciarum duodecim. Quadraginta igitur pondo libras triginta nunc faciunt unciarum sedecim singulas, more nostro. Ego autem foenum compressum, sicut solet in magnis foenilibus esse postquam exaruit, curiose dimensus, inveni mensuram cubiti solidi paulo plus quam pondo quadraginta foeni continere. Propterea cubum unum foeni (cubitalem semper intelligo) in capita boum singula distribui quotidie, nimium esset. Hac enim longa dieta, saginarentur supra modum. Nam (ut ait Aristoteles) omnia animalia, & praecipue quibus venter est calidus, quiete, immotioneque pinguescunt. Nil itaque dubito, quin singulis bobus ociosis in diem sufficeret dimidium cubi, hoc est foeni pondo viginti. Sed ut contentiosis etiam ora compescam, volo cubum foeni singulatim in capita dari quotidie. Boves ergo quadringenti totidem cubos sumptu diurno capientes, absumunt anni spatio cubos; centum quadraginta sex millia. Iam vero supra disposui medium in arca tabulatum, decem cubitis a supremo distare. Ubi etiam apothecas pabulorum, atque frugum omnis generis collocavi. Nunc autem ponamus illam arcae partem duobus his tabulatis interceptam, totam esse pratensi foeno refertam. Cum igitur sit foenilis istius trecentum cubitorum longitudo, quinquaginta cubitorum latitudo, & altitudo cubitorum decem, /23/ summa fit in corpus cubitalium cuborum, centum quinquaginta millia. Qui numerus annuum sumptum foeni pro quadragentis bobus quatuor cuborum millibus excedit. Ex his itaque cernere datur, medianam hanc contignationem non solum satis esse, sed etiam exuberare quadrupedum alimentis. etiam si altero tanto plures essent. Inter quas & reptilia grandiora collocavi, ut pote dracones, cocodrillos, hippopotamos, vitulos marinos, serpentes boas. Caetera autem corpore natura formavit exigua, veluti viperas, angues, aspides, cerastas, hydras, basiliscos, lacertas praeterea virides, aliasque minusculas, stelliones, cameleontes, salamandras, quibus tantus rigor, ut ignem tactum extinguant non alio modo quam glacies. Haec autem, & si quae sunt id genus alia, circa stabulationes cavernulis vel intra materiem perforatis, recipi commode potuerunt. Canum porro genus omne circa culinam unde pascuntur habitasse putandum est, quo nullum frequentius animal sordes suas vomitat, easdemque remandit. Et tam sibi, quam aliis rabie perniciosa vexatur. Propterea videntur canes haereticorum typum in arca praetulisse.

XXI. De Contignatione Tertia.

IAM in cotabulatione suprema habitationes hominum, volucrumque omnium, cum apothecis, cibisque necessariis collocavi, nulla numeratione, distinctioneque generum facta, per loculos dimensos, viasque separantes, sicut in stabulatione quadrupedum ordinavi. Cuius sane rei necessitas in hac quidem parte nulla est. Sed reddenda potius ratio, cur tanta loci magnitudo rebus tam modicis adhibeatur. Quamvis enim sit varium volatile genus, & aeque multiplex propemodum quadrupedum generi: adeo tamen & corporatura, & commeatuum, habitandique ratione differunt, ut vix (etiam aestimatore maligno) dici possint volucres gradientium quinquagesimae partis. Sed cum omnes quadrupedes tabulatum primum exceperit: /24/ sequens autem pabulum ipsorum, quod reliquum fuit bipedum genus ponendum erat in reliquo. Quamquam non est incredibile ipsum Noe futuri praescium, omnia scilicet corruptum iri cataclysmo, copiosam suppellectilem, tam rusticam, quam urbanam, ferramentorumque genus omne fabrilium, locis vacantibus reposuisse. Si vero necesse fuit in arca servari pisces amphibiis in cibum, avibusque piscariis, compingi piscina potuit in hac parte, eo quo supra dictum est modo. Et Ctesibiana machina, aliove quolibet pneumaticae rationis hydraulo facile repleri, sublataque per sistulam papilla depleri. Nunc igitur disputationis nostrae cursu eo perventum existimo, ut super cubitis symmetriarum sesquipedalibus, nullus ultra scrupulus relinquatur, quin ad universale viventium semen ab inundatione servandum in arca largissime sufficient. Cuius scenographiam secundum dicta prius hic apposui.

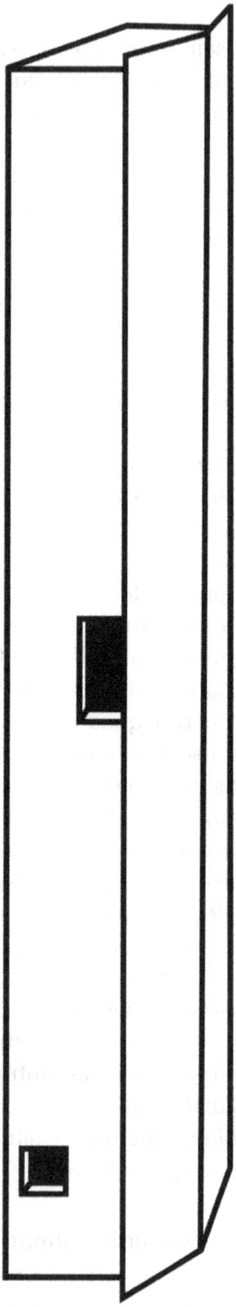

XXII. De Novem Pedum Cubitis Quomodo Processerit Error.

NON SATIS erit fortasse sesquipedali mensura cubitum rationibus multis, & opere probasse, nisi & sexquiplo maiores, hoc est novem pedum cubitos inveterata iam multorum opinione receptos confutavero. Quam ab Origenis expositione male percepta profectam invenio. Is enim homilia secunda super arcae fabrica loquitur in hunc sensum. His omnibus tanta arte compositis obiiciunt quidam quaestiones, & praecipue

Appelles qui fuit discipulus quidem Marcionis, sed alterius haereseos magis quam eius quam a magistro suscepit inventor. Is ergo dum assignare cupit scripta Moysis nihil in se divinae sapientiae, nihilque operis sancti spiritus continere, exaggerat huiusmodi dicta, & dicit, nullo genere fieri potuisse ut tam breve spatium tot animalium genera, eorumque cibos, qui per totum annum sufficerent capere potuisset. Quomodo (inquit) fieri potuit istud spatium quod scriptum est? ut quatuor saltem solos elephantos capere potuerit. Et post ea addit. Constat ergo fictam esse fabulam. Quod si est, constat non esse a Deo hanc scripturam. Sed ad haec nos quae a prudentibus viris, & hebraicarum traditionum gnaris, atque a veteribus magistris didicimus, ad auditorum noticiam deferemus. Aiebant ergo maiores, quae Moyses qui (ut de eo scriptura testatur) omni sapientia Aegyptiorum fuerit eruditus, secundum artem geometricam, quam praecipue Aegyptii callent, cubitorum numerum in hoc loco posuit. Apud geometras enim secundum eam rationem, quae apud eos virtus vocatur, ex solido & quadrato vel in sex cubitos unus deputatur, si generaliter: vel trecentos, si minutatim deducatur. Quae utique ratio si observetur in huius arcae mensura: invenientur & longitudinis, & latitudinis tanta spatia, quae vere totius mundi reparanda germina, & universarum animantium capere rediviva semina potuerint. Haec quantum ad historiae pertinet rationem adversus eos dicta sint, qui impugnare scripturas veteris testamenti nituntur, tanquam impossibilia quaedam, & irrationabilia continentes. Sic habet ad literam latinus interpres. Nam authoris graeca non extant. Sanctus autem Augustinus /25/ vir in literis sacris eruditione praecipuus, libro quaestionum super Genesim locum hunc ita prosequitur. Quaestionem (inquit) istam cubito geometrico solvit Origines, asserens non frustra scriptura dixisse, quod Moyses omni sapientia Aegyptiorum fuerit eruditus, qui geometricam dilexerunt. Cubitum autem geometricum dixit tantum valere, quantum nostra cubita sex valent. Si ergo tam magna cubita intelligamus: nulla quaestio est tantae capacitatis arcam fuisse, ut posset illa omnia continere. Haec Augustinus, cuius authoritatem, quod merito magna sit, omnes quotquot viderim tractantes ista sequuntur. In quibus & ipse fui, donec re perspecta diligentius, ipsa me veritatem geometria docuit. Qua qui sunt destituti, nihil est mirum in istis errare, cum sint a sensu communi valde remota. Si enim ex hoc Origenis loco cubiti longitudinem simpliciter extenderis in sex: itidem & unum extendam in trecentos, cum utrumque dixerit author. Sed hoc postremum, tam impudenter ausus est dicere nemo. Et secundum extensionem huiusmodi res eo deducetur, ut idem cubitus maior sit, & minor. Quod est absurdum. Videndum igitur quanam discretione sensus, propositum stare possit, utroque modo. Iam in praecedentibus ostendi, arcae solidum continere cubitales cubos quatercentum quinquaginta millia. Planum est insuper arcae longitudinem suae latitudinis fieri sexcuplum. Basis igitur arcae in sex aequalia quadrata dividi potest, quorum commune latus est cubitorum quinquaginta, quod in se multiplicando facies cubitos quadratos, duo millia quingentos, id erit embadon unius sex quadratorum in basi. Rursum multiplicando cubitos quadrati duo millia quingentos, in triginta cubitos altitudinis, fient septingenta quinque millia cubitalium cuborum. Quae est sexta pars corporis arcae. Ergo ut ait Origenes unusquisque talium cubitorum deputatur in sex. Quoniam sexies septingenta quinque millia cubitalium cuborum, summam quatercentum quinquaginta millium constituunt. Quae est arcae capacitas, eadem quam per meum ante calculum inveni. Alteram propositi partem unum scilicet cubitum in trecentos deputari, sic ostendo. Accipe alterutrum ex minoribus arcae planis, cuius unum latus est cubitorum triginta, alterum vero quinquaginta: haec inter se duo latera multiplicatione, cubita quadrata mille quingenta producunt. Quem numerum multiplicans iterum in tertiam arcae dimensionem trecentum cubitorum, ex uno quoque minutatim cubito quadrato, trecentos solidos efficies, & in summam, quatercentum quinquaginta millia. Id autem est solidum arcae, sicut prius. Quod erat demonstrandum. Et ita secundum rationem geometricam, ex solido & quadrato verum habet Origenis dictum, utroque modo. Non autem quod cubitus geometricus tantum valeat, quantum sex nostra cubita valent, ut asserit Augustinus. Nec cubito geometrico, sed cubicatione geometrica quaestionem solvit Origenes. Cum non cubitos geometres, sed cubicationem habeat seorsum ab usu communi. Istius modi cubitorum multiplicatio, verum etiam habebit in prismate, atque pyramide, & universaliter ad omne corpus, cui possit aequale fieri solidum parallelepipedon, super basi quae sit huic quam habet arca similis. Animadvertendum tamen in hoc Origenis proposito, illud esse vitiosum maxime, quod res cum alias per se tum artis ingenio difficilis, aenigmate quodam affectato verborum, & involucro sic obscura-/26/tur, ut divinare magis oporteat, quam interpretari. Planum enim, & secundum naturam erat dicere, numeros istos cubitorum in descriptione positos, rationibus geometricis inveniri, capacitatem quatercentum quinquaginta millium cubitorum in corpus efficere. Huiusmodi praeterea novempedalis extensio cubitorum recepta communiter, sicut dubium capacitatis artem non intelligentibus aufert, ita & intelligentibus vastitatem enormem, & absurdum operis infert. Iam enim supra demonstravi arcae magnitudinem sesquipedalibus cubitorum modulis constitutam, ad animalium omnium conservanda genera, annuosque commeatus comportandos abunde sufficere. Si autem supponatur arca fieri similis forma priori, sed novem pedum cubitis modulata erit ipsa quidem sexcuplo longior, latior, & altior altera. Corpore vero ducenties decies sexcies capacior. Quandoquidem similium corporum inter se ratio est, laterum eiusdem rationis triplicata. Verum, si quis ex geometricis elementis ista non capiat: numeratione sic inveniet. Quoniam cubitus novem pedum, sesquipedalem cubitum sexcies in se continet. Longitudo igitur arcae maioris cubitos sesquipedales habebit mille octingentos, latitudo trecentos, altitudo centum octoginta. Quos numeros inter se multiplicando, sicut cubicatione priori factum est, summam conficies 97200000, hoc est nonagesies septies millies mille & ducenta millia cubitalium cuborum, quae est capacitas istius arcae maioris. Quam partiendo in minoris alterius arcae cubos quater centum quinquaginta millia, videbis ipsam in maiore contineri quoties antea dixi. Esset igitur arca secundum novem pedum cubitos ducenties quindecies maior quam oporteat. Ita ut plusquam una tota arca aequalis priori singulis boum paribus attribuatur. Quo nihil esse potest magis absurdum. Ad haec etiam dico: si giganteos huiusmodi cubitos receperis: ad fabulas quidem prope res rediit. Nulla si quidem opis humanae facultate tam vastae molis aedificium navigationis, onerumque patiens constituti mihi posse videtur. Neque enim omnia (ut ait Vitruvius) eisdem rationibus agi possunt, nec modum quemlibet incrementi opera recipiunt: sed aut nimium crescendo dilabuntur, aut explicationem prorsus non habent. His itaque perpensis diligenter, cubitos istos sexcuplices, nulla ratione fundatos, opus nostrum perdere magis quam probare quis iam non videat? De quibus ipse etiam Augustinus non omnino sibi confidere visus est, libro decimo quinto de civitate Dei, ubi solutionem quaestionis aliam afferre conatur, sic inquiens. Qui dicunt non potuisse capere arcae illius quantitatem animalium genera tam multa, hi mihi videntur non computare nisi trecenta cubita longitudinis, & latitudinis quinquaginta, & triginta altitudinis, nec cogitare aliud tantum esse in superioribus, itemque aliud tantum in superioribus superiorum, ac per hoc ter ducta illa cubita fieri nongenta per longum, centum quinquaginta per latum, nonaginta per altum. Ex hoc Augustinus nil aliud infert quam tria in opere tabulata ipsi basi parallela intelligi debere, sicut antea disposui: quae veluti tres arcas particulares divisione sua faciant. Et ita arcae longitudo triplicatur. De latitudine vero, & altitudine quod eodem modo simul fiant triplices (ut ipse ait). Id omnino falsum est. Sic enim alicuius partes corporis, maiores essent suo toto. Quod est impossibile. Verissime tamen ex hoc arguitur illorum computatio ridicula, qui citra planum & solidum dimensione sola linearum, corpus attendunt. Quod perinde valet, ac si /27/ quis verborum sensus solis notarum lineamentis, nihil aliud intelligendo requirat. Verum ea fuit semper haereticorum perversitas, ut quae non intelligunt pertinacissime cavillentur, nec ullis rationibus cedant. Sed maledictis potius insectentur eos a quibus de veritate dissentiunt. Quod sum expertus in quibusdam aliquando mecum super hac disputatione congressis. Nam genus fere nullum est ex damnatis olim, & explosis erroribus, quod non aliqua ex parte nunc revocetur in medium. Et quod in novis astruendis ingenium negat: in veteribus afferendis pertinacia supplet. Ex quibus aliud aliis placet, nec quicquam tamen omnibus unum. Nusquam enim sibi congruit malitia. Et haec de cubitis quae falso dicuntur ab arte. Qua prorsus non erat opus ad obiectum tam indocti cavillatoris. Quid enim ceco cum speculo? Vel graculo cum fidibus? Ut habet paroemia vetus. Libet itaque nunc exarmato mihi congredi cum hoste, etiam stipato suis elephantis. Quid ais o Maricionita? Quid in arcam domini haeretice garris? Immo barris, cum beluis istis non Aphris, aut Indicis, sed plane monstrificis, quibus dum arcam solis quatuor imples, non arcam bestiae modicam, sed immodicas facit bestias arca, commentumque tuum belvinum equo Troiano fabulosius reddit. Nam si quatuor saltem solos elephantos (ut tu exaggeras) capere non possit: altitudinem in singulis cubitorum plusquam triginta confingis, longitudinem vero decuplo maiorem, cum crassitudine cubitorum plusquam duodecim. Ubi non tam magnitudinis prodigio, quam deformitatis vitio peccas; cum sit ista corporatura draconibus propior, quam elephantis. Quos si disponas aliter, eadem quae prius altitudo, cum sexta longitudinis parte manebit, obtinebitque singulorum crassitudo quartum aedifici partem. Cui portento quid simile dicam, non invenio. Constat igitur (ut tuis in te verbis concludam) fictam esse non capacitatis nostrae, sed stabulationis tuae fabulam. Est itaque quod tu negas, & res ipsa probat a Deo scriptura prophetae, tua vero, sicut ostendis, a Sathana patre, qui te, tuique similes generavit. Sed iam Momum istum sua sibi montra fabricantem relinquamus. Et praeter eam quam in praecedentibus explicavi formam operis, alias aliorum quales sint dispicamus.

XXIII. De Variis Arcae Figuris, & Earum Scenographia.

MOSIS descriptionem interpretati doctores basim eandem omnes intelligunt, specie scilicet (ut ante dixi) rectangula, altera parte longiore sexcies altera. Sed in superstructione fundamenti quatuor fere modis inter se variis aedificant. Nam Origenes homilia supradicta, Arcam (inquit) ego puto, quantum ex his quae describuntur apparet, quatuor angulis ex imo consurgentibus, eisdemque paulatim usque ad summum in angustum arctatis, in spatium unius cubiti fuisse collectam. Ita ut cubitus sit longitudo, & latitudo cacuminis. Haec authoris descriptio nihil aliud esset quam pyramis absciso vertice, si planum sectionis non quadratum, sed altera parte sexies longius esset. Alii porro multi satis Hugonem sequentes, arcae dimidium altitudine cubitorum quindecim in sua basi collocarunt, reliquos totidem pyrami-/28/dato fastigio, verticeque mutilo Origenis more complentes. Hanc autem sic dimidiatam altitudinem quidam improbantes, totum arcae corpus ad suos triginta cubitos erectum decacuminata pyramide similiter contegunt. Nulla tamen altitudinis istius testudinatae mensura constituta. Novissime autem recentiores aliqui, quorum est Caietanus, arcam nostram ea corporis specie transfigurant, quod a geometris prisma vocatur. Cuius duo ex opposito plana parallela, super minoribus basis lateribus, sint trigona verticibus abscisis, latitudine cubitali, reliqua vero tria plana parallelogramma. Huiusmodi formas praeter id quod ordinationi prophetae non plene respondent, alia etiam non pauca reprobant. Primum enim pseudopyramis ista Origenis, atque etiam prisma Caietani, quid habent cum arca simile? Talis etiam cacuminis quadrata deformatio, vel deformitas potius non solum est aspectu foeda, sed etiam inutilis operi, de qua rationem nullam congruentem dicere possis. Et ipsa tota pyramis modum fabricationis habet impeditum, atque difficilem: & quo nullus ad stabulationem animalium magis ineptus, nec excogitari quidem possit. Ad navigationem vero quod inutilia sint haec corpora, communis navigiorum dispositio satis ostendit. In quibus semper id quod est contractum vergit in carinam, & immergitur aquis, summa autem latitudo prodit in apertum, & supra fluitat. Pyramis igitur, & prisma nisi statuantur inverso corpore, ut sit infra vertex, fundus vero supra nihil super natabit, sed totum submergetur. Ex capacitate autem quam supra demonstravi necessariam, tertia pars solum, nec etiam tota remanebit in pyramide. In prismate vero paululum aliquid supra dimidium. Habet tamen haec prima constitutio tam absurda assensores aliquot (quorum fuit is cuius interpretatio dicitur interlinearis) rationem frivolam omnino praeposteramque sequentes. Qua & Origenes formam suam ipse commendat, inquiens: Quantum ad necessitatem pluviarum diluvii spectat, nulla potuit tam conveniens, & congrua arcae species dari, quam ut e summo, velut e tecto quodam in angustum culmine ducto diffunderet imbrium ruinas. Hoc ego iam a principio reprobavi satis, ubi fastigium cubitale tecto sufficere probatum est. Sed ecce dum pluviae guttas isti formidant, in fluctus profundos sese demergunt. In tertia vero figura, quam Hugo cum arca dimidiatam, atque testudine dividuam facit, nihil sane est aliud quam cum vero miscere falsum. Unde etiam quod bonum erat, mali societate vitiatur. Cum enim ipsa pyramidata constructio etiam super basi solida modum habeat (sicut dixi) perplexum, atque difficilem tum longe molestius, & operosius erit, atque etiam deterius fiet, si super arcae dimidio collocetur. Ipsa namque dissimilium corporum, & contra se pugnantium commissura, nisi colligationibus robustis, crebrisque transversariis, & erismatum fulturis validissime distineatur, pars inferior pondere, violentiaque testudinis tota protrudetur. Et huiusmodi catenationes multo plus oneris, & impedimenti navigio praestant, quam bona vecturae pars. Talis praeterea commistio praeter id quod opus corrumpit, parte etiam fere tertia quantitatem ab arca detrahit. In qua sane perquirenda dum opus suum recenseret Hugo non alioquin ἀγεωμετριτος satis sese diu frustraque fatigavit, multa super trigonis, catheris, hypotenusis, diametris, tetragonicisque lateribus inculcans. Unde cum se non posset extricare, nec idoneum exitum inveniret, longuam suam disputationem ita concludit. In trigonis his /29/ /30/ (inquit) & tetragonis, multa alia

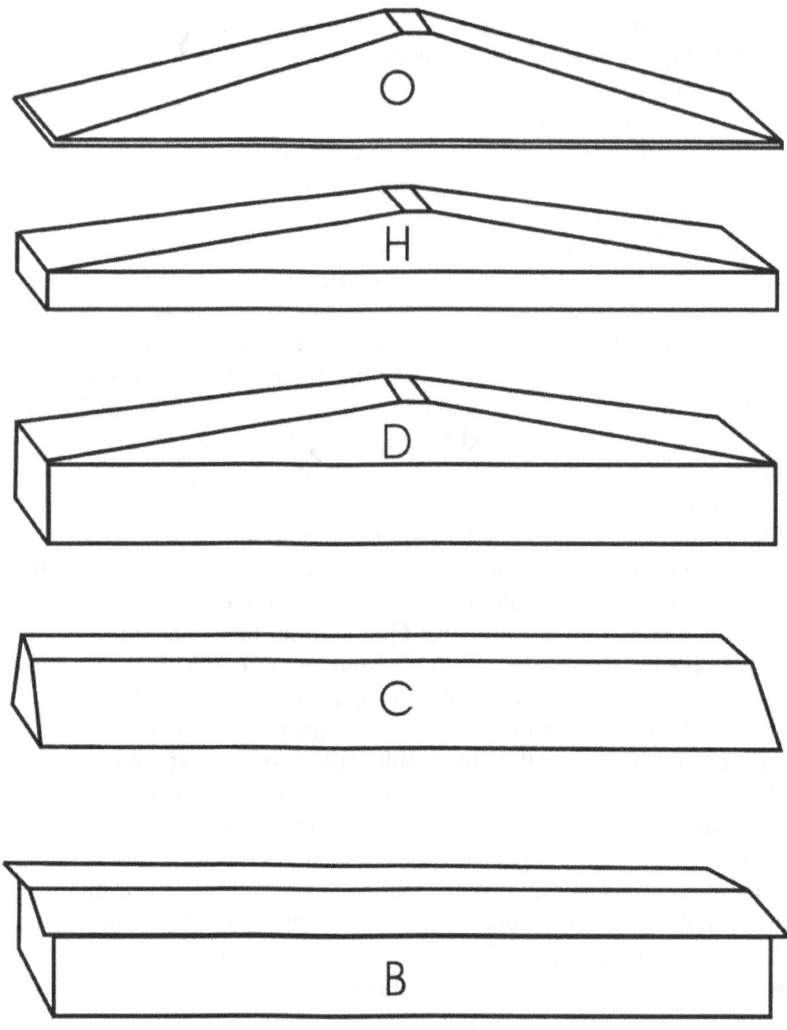

O. Arcae forma secundum Origenem. H. secundum Hugonem.
D. secundum aliquos doctores. C. secundum Caietanum.
B. secundum Buteonem.

invenies ad subtilitatem geometricae disciplinae pertentia, quae omnia nos propter fastidium declinamus. Sed plane declinationem istam a proposito, non tam fastidium quam imperitia fecit. Nam in ipso calculo primum turpiter errat, dicens, diametrum basis in arca, & ut ipse vocat diagonium esse longuam cubitos trecentum quatuor cum semisse cubiti. Quod non ita est, cum sit ipsa diametros, tetragonicum latus 92500. quodquidem trecentis quatuor cubitis & quadrante brevius est. Nihil itaque mirum si nobis Hugo suae domus interiora non ostendit, quin in ipso statim limine pedem impegit. In quarta demum constructione figuram ex praescripto, nomenque suum obtinet arca tota praeter operculum, quod super ea quae iam notavi vitia testudinis, non magis error, quam temeritas authorum facit asymmetron. Supradictarum autem quatuor formarum scenographias hic apposui, quibus & meam adiunxi. Super qua iam disputatione multa satis, & sensum meum comprobasse, & calumnias hereticorum confutasse videor. Caeterum si in erroribus aliquorum notandis meos ipse fortassis, ut homo, protulerim, in his asserendis nihil ago pertinaciter, sed orthodoxorum sententiae totum me plane subiicio. Absit enim procul a me, ut arcam Domini corpoream quantum potui diligenter perscrutatus, ab ea cuius fuit ipsa typus, hoc est ab ecclesia sancta catholica diversum quicquam, aut dissonam adstruere velim. Et in hoc habeat suum finem commentatio nostra.

References

Allard, G. 1970 [1797]. *Bibliothèque de Dauphiné*. Slatkine Reprints, Geneva.

Allen, D.C. 1963. *The Legend of Noah*. University of Illinois Press, Urbana, IL.

Anonymous. 1753. *Bibliotheque Raisonée des Ouvrages des Savans de l'Europe Tome Vingt-Deux*. J. Wetstein & G. Smith, Amsterdam.

Aristotle . 1965. *Historia Animalium*. Trans. A.L. Peck. Harvard University Press, Cambridge, MA.

Athenaeus. 1854. *The Deipnosophists or Banquet of the Learned of Athenaeus* Volume I. Trans. C.D. Yonge. Henry G. Bohn, London.

Augustine and. 1995. On the Lord's Epiphany. In: Rotelle, J.E. ed. *The Works of Saint Augustine: A Translation for the 21st Century, Sermons, (341-400) on Various Subjects*, Volume 3. Trans. E. Hill. New City Press, Brooklyn, NY.

Augustine. 1996. Sermo CCCLXXIII De Epiphania Domini, I. In: Migne, J. *Patrologia Latina*, Volume 39. Chadwyck-Healey Inc., Alexandria, VA.

Augustine. 2004. City of God. Trans. M. Dods. In: Schaff, P. ed. *Nicene and Post Nicene Fathers*, Volume 2. Hendrickson Publishers, Peabody, MA.

Bayle, P. 1820 [1739]. *Dictionnaire Historique et Critique Nouvelle Édition Tome Quatrième*. Desoer, Paris.

Buteo, J. 1556. *Logistica*. Apud Gulielmum Rouillium, Lugduni.

Brand, L. 2006. A biblical perspective on the philosophy of science. *Origins (GRI)* 59:6-42.

Caesar, 1904. *Caesar's Commentaries on the Gallic War*. Trans. by publisher. Lee & Shepard, Boston.

Caietani, T. de V. 1639. *Opera Omnia Quotquot in Sacrae Scripturae Expositionem Reperiuntur Tomus Primus*. Sumpt. Iacobi & Petri Prost, Lyons.

Cantor, M. 1900. *Vorlesungen über Geschichte der Mathematik Zweiter Band*. B.G. Teubner, Leipzig.

Chorier, N. 1672. *Histoire Generale de Dauphiné*. Chez Iean Thioly, Lyon.

Cicero. 1908. De Lege Agraria Oratio Secunda. In: Mueller, C.F.W., *Scripta Que Manserunt Omnia*, Part II Vol. II. Aedibus B.G. Teubneri,

Lipsiae.

Cicero. 2001. *On Moral Ends*. Trans. Raphael Woolf. Cambridge University Press, Cambridge.

Cohn, N. 1996. *Noah's Flood: The Genesis Story in Western Thought*. Yale University Press, New Haven, CT.

Columella. 1941. *On Agriculture*, Volume 1. Trans. H. B. Ash. Harvard University Press, Cambridge, MA.

Copernicus, N. 1543. *De Revolutionibus Orbium Coelestium*. Ioh. Petreium, Nuremberg.

Cummings, V.M. 1972. *Noah's Ark: Fact or Fable?* Creation-Science Research Center, San Diego.

Drake, S., ed. 1957. *Discoveries and Opinions of Galileo*. Anchor Books, New York.

Drexel, J. 1640. *Noe Architectus Arcae in Dluvio Navarchus Descriptus et Morali Doctrina Illustratus*. Io. Cnobbari, Antwerp.

Freedman, H., and M. Simon, eds. 1939. *Midrash Rabbah Genesis* Volume 1. Trans. H. Freedman. Soncino Press, London.

Hoefer, J.C.F. 1855. *Nouvelle Biographie Générale Tome Septième*. Firmin Didot Frères, Paris.

Hugh. 1962. *Hugh of Saint-Victor: Selected Spiritual Writings*. Trans. Community of St. Mary the Virgin (CSMV). Faber and Faber, London.

Hugo de S. Victore 1996. De Arca Noe Morali Libri IV. In: Migne, J., ed. Patrologia Latina. Chadwyck-Healey Inc., Alexandria, VA.

Irenaeus. 1885. Against Heresies. In Coxe, A.C. ed. *The Apostolic Fathers with Justin Martyr and Irenaeus*. Christian Literature Publishing Company, Buffalo, NY, pp.309-567.

Josephus, F. 1987. *The Antiquities of the Jews*, 2nd edition. Trans. W. Whiston. Hendrickson Publishers, Inc., Peabody, MA.

Karpinski, L.C. and F.W. Kokomoor. 1928. The teaching of elementary geometry in the seventeenth century. *Isis* 10(1):21-32.

Kircher, A. 1675. *Arca Noë in Tres Libros Digesta*. Joannem Janssonium, Amsterdam.

Kloyda, M.T.A.K. 1937. Linear and quadratic equations 1550-1660. *Osiris* 3(1):165-192.

Kokomoor, F.W. 1928. The distinctive features of seventeenth century geometry. *Isis* 10(2):367-415.

Lynch, J.M. 2002. 'Follies of the present day': Scriptural Geology from 1817 to 1857. In: J.M. Lynch, ed. *Creationism and Scriptural Geology*. Vol. 1. Thoemmes Press, Bristol, pp. ix-xxiv.

Michaud Frères. 1812. *Biographie Universelle, Ancienne et Moderne Tome Sixième*. Michaud Frères, Paris.

Maggi, H. 1564. *Variarum Lectionum seu Miscellaneorum Libri IIII*. Iordani Zileti, Venice.

Montucla, J.F. 1799. *Histoire des Mathématiques Tome Premier*. Henri Agasse, Paris.

Moreri, L. 1759. *Le Grande Dictionaire*. 20th edition. Les Libraires Associés, Paris.

Navarra, F. 1974. *Noah's Ark: I Touched It.* Logos International, Plainfield, NJ.

Origen. 1982. Genesis Homily II. In: Heine, R.E. trans. *Homilies on Genesis and Exodus.* The Catholic University of America Press, Washington, DC.

Pliny the Elder. 1857. *The Natural History of Pliny.* Trans. J. Bostock and H. T. Riley. Henry G. Bohn, London.

Rex, W.E. 1976. "Arche de Noé" and other religious articles by Abbé Mallet in the *Encyclopédie. Eighteenth-Century Studies* 9(3):333-352.

Roberts, J.H. 1988. *Darwinism and the Divine in America.* University of Notre Dame Press, Notre Dame, Indiana.

Schott, G. 1677. *Magiae universalis naturae et artis.* Bamburg.

Smith, J.P. 1840. *On the Relation between the Holy Scriptures and Some Parts of Geological Science.* D. Appleton & Co., New York.

Taylor, C. 1832. *Calmet's Dictionary of the Holy Bible.* Holdsworth and Ball, London.

de Thou, J.-A. 1740. *Histoire Universelle Tome Troisieme.* Henri Scheurleer, the Hague.

de Thou, J.-A. and A. Teissier. 1696. *Les Éloges des Hommes Scavans.* F. Halma, Utrecht.

Varro, M.T. 1938. *On the Latin Language,* Volume 1. Trans. R. G. Kent. Harvard University Press, Cambridge, MA.

Verdonk, J.J. 1981. Buteo, Johannes. In Gillispie, C.C., ed. *Dictionary of Scientific Biography Volume 1.* Charles Scribner's Sons, New York, p. 618.

Vesalius, A. 1543. *De Humani Corporis Fabrica.* Johannes Oporinus, Basel.

Vitruvius. 1874. *The Architecture of Marcus Vitruvius Pollio in Ten Books* (Second Edition). Trans. J. Gwilt. Lockwood & Co. London.

Vossii, G.I. 1660. *Quatuor Artibus Popularibus, de Philologia et Scientiis Mathematicis.* Ioannis Blaev, Amsterdam.

Wilkins, J. 1668. *An Essay Towards a Real Character and a Philosophical Language.* Sa. Gellibrand and John Martyn, London.

Wilkins, J. 1802. *The Mathematical and Philosophical Works of the Right Rev. John Wilkins.* 2nd ed. Vol . 1. C. Whittingham, London.

Wood, T.C. 2007. Bishop John Wilkins, F.R.S. (1614-1672) and his discussion of Noah's Ark. *Occasional Papers of the BSG* 9:1-9.

Woodmorappe, J. 1996. *Noah's Ark: A Feasibility Study.* Institute for Creation Research, El Cajon, CA.

Young, D.A. 1995. *The Biblical Flood: A Case Study of the Church's Response to Extrabiblical Evidence.* Eerdmans, Grand Rapids, MI.

Buteo Bibliography

1554. *Opera Geometrica*. Lyons.
1558. *Orationes Graecorum veteres ad Deum et Sanctos*. Lyons.
1559. *Logistica, quae et arithmetica vulgo dicitur in libros quinque digesta*. Lyons.
1559. *De quadratura circuli libri duo*. Lyons.
1562. *Apologia adversus epistolam Jacobi Peletarii depravatoris Elementorum Euclidis*. Lyons.

Index

CORE Issues in Creation

Established in 2005, the *CORE Issues* monograph series presents high quality scholarly work from or related to a young-age creation perspective. This monograph series is not for the publication of scholarly critiques of alternative positions (other venues exist for that kind of publication). Rather, *CORE Issues* has been created to publish any monograph in any discipline (philosophy, theology, physics, geology, biology, archaeology, linguistics, etc., etc.) which substantially contributes to the systematic development of a positive, young-age creation model. Original monographs will thoroughly review the conventional and creationist literature on the subject, offer a constructive interpretation of the subject's data, integrate well with other disciplines as the model is constructed, and advance creation model development. Other monographs offer reprints, compendia, or translations of significant historical works that are currently unavailable. *CORE Issues* is peer-reviewed and will strive for the very highest scholarship standards. *CORE Issues* is a joint publication of the Center for Origins Research at Bryan College and Wipf & Stock Publishers.

CORE Issues does not publish works written only by Bryan College faculty but encourages outside submissions. Researchers may submit monograph proposals (full manuscripts are not accepted) to CORE either electronically at info@bryancore.org or by regular mail:

CORE Issues editor
Bryan College 7802
721 Bryan Drive
Dayton, TN 37321

Previous Volumes in the *CORE Issues* Series

1. A Creationist Review and Preliminary Analysis of the History, Geology, Climate, and Biology of the Galápagos Islands, by Wood (2005)
2. Johannes Buteo's The Shape and Capacity of Noah's Ark, trans. by Griffith & Monette (2008)

www.ingramcontent.com/pod-product-compliance
Lightning Source LLC
Chambersburg PA
CBHW071106090426
42737CB00013B/2510

* 9 7 8 1 5 5 6 3 5 8 7 1 5 *